A Recipe for Magic

By Julia Sotas Mattis

With Major Contributions
by Gary M. Douglas and Dr. Dain Heer

A Recipe for Magic

ISBN (paperback): 978-1-63493-756-6

ISBN (eBook): 978-1-63493-757-3

The author and publisher of the book do not make any claim or guarantee for any physical, mental, emotional, spiritual, or financial result. All products, services and information provided by the author are for general education and entertainment purposes only. The information provided herein is in no way a substitute for medical advice. In the event you use any of the information contained in this book for yourself, the author and publisher assume no responsibility for your actions.

Published by Access Consciousness® Publishing

www.acpublishing.com

ACKNOWLEDGEMENTS

To Gary: For always being there

To Dain: For being so relentlessly brave

To Anthony: For making life wonderful

To Grace: For so poignantly naming this book

To the amazing Amanda Holland: For being the person who gave this book life and made it what it is today

What are the greatest possibilities available for your future?

Gary Douglas

TABLE OF CONTENTS

FOREWORD

Have you ever heard the saying, ask and you shall receive? How many times have you thought that was crazy, and getting what you wanted had to be hard?

What if it was just that easy?

Julia is the perfect example of having that mystical energy show up every day. Creating above and beyond what it means to work hard to achieve goals. Her determination, resilience and unwavering demand to have and inspire more consciousness and magic in the world has been focused and nothing short of inspirational.

Now, she's giving you her secrets and tips on how to make that happen for you too.

With a sprinkling of magic and a touch of your own fairy dust, you can make anything happen. Julia is the perfect person to guide you through, and this book makes it as easy as asking and receiving.

~ Grace Douglas

INTRODUCTION

If there was ever a time in your life when you knew, just knew that there was more, or should be more, or could be more, and you wondered why on earth you weren't getting it, you are in the right place.

If you have ever felt that you are living in two conflicting worlds – one where you are being told that very little is possible, and one where everything is possible, and you'd really like to know what it takes to quit the former and live in the latter, you are also in the right place.

I've spent my life looking for the world where everything is possible. I looked for it seemingly everywhere. Then I found out that the world of possibility I had been seeking was with me all along. In fact, it was me. I just needed some better tools to navigate my own capacities.

This book is about one of the most potent tools I've used to work with the universe and all its wonders --- the very simply named "Energy Pull." And because I just can't help myself, I've also packed this book with a whole lot of other cool tools to add to your magic toolkit along the way.

The energy pull was a "secret recipe" that was given to me many moons ago when I came across Access Consciousness®. In truth, the energy pull is not truly a secret. I myself have been yelling it joyfully from the rooftops and talking about it non-stop for many years, as have many wonderful and empowering people around me, including Gary Douglas, the wonderful friend who first gave me this tool. It is funny how often people don't hear it, though. Or they hear about it, but they don't take it upon themselves to change their life with it.

Perhaps it is because the recipe is too simple, too basic, that people think it just can't be that easy!

Well, what if it was?

What if there was a way to get everything you want – and greater – with such incredible ease it'll astound and delight you?

Sometimes it is hard to switch into that mental gear of trusting that anything really is possible if you just ask for it. I hear you. I get you. And, I'm still going to tell you that it is possible.

I am going to temper my claim – it is easy, it is simple --- AND you also have to be willing to work at learning to receive what you ask for.

A friend of mine once said if you are going to ask the universe for anything, you have to ask for at least double of what you really want, because you already think you are too greedy, grubby, miserable and awful to get what you want, so you'll only ever accept about half of your request.

Therefore, the target of this book is two-fold. I'm going to share with you, to the best of my ability, the power of the Energy Pull, and how to do it with ease. I'm also going to take a deep dive into some of the core areas of desire in our lives – money, business, bodies and relationships – and talk about the barriers we put up to receiving what we ask for in these areas, and of course how to begin melting them. Because recognising that we have a lot of judgements and beliefs that stop the magic from rolling in is also a huge part of this game.

And I believe it should be a game. This whole process should be a grand adventure, otherwise why would you do it in the first place?

I would also like to ask you a couple of questions before we get started:

First, are you willing to have the adventure of trusting in you?

Second, will you indulge me, as I take you back a little and set the scene for how this all began for me? I have lived an unusual life, and I'm always excited about who else can come play with me on this bold undertaking. I hope as we go along in this book, you will come to the place where you realise that you are not alone and that we are all on this amazing planet, doing this together.

I would love to live in a world where everyone truly knows that anything you ask for, you can have. And it can be so much more fun and wondrous than you've ever imagined.

PART ONE

CHAPTER 1
The Seeker

Hi.

I'm Julia. And I'm very fucking weird.

The energy I create my life with – the wonderment, magic and reaching for awareness beyond the "norm" – started from as early as I can remember.

I grew up on a farm in rural Canada and from an early age I realised that I saw the world very differently from those around me.

At five years old I would trek through the kitchen and wonder, "If I turn right, is that my destiny and there is no other path, or did I turn right by choice? What would happen if I turned left? What different possibility would show up if I did? Do I have the ability to turn left?"

Fortunately, I was born into a wacky family, with an outlandish mother who helped me explore a wide range of modalities and questions. She taught me about ghosts, healing light, and how to talk to my body. My father wasn't quite as versed in these particular fields of awareness and energy, but he was a great financial advisor, with stacks of books on stock investing, retirement planning and world economics. He educated my sister and I on financial responsibility and was a goofy, fun and loving dad.

My mom, Elly, is a boundless, glorious radical in her artistic outlets. She was a costume designer and seamstress, and I spent many nights falling asleep to the sound of her sewing machine, her endless enthusiasm wafting from her sewing room across the hall. Mom also had a rainbow of eccentric friends who were artists, healers, and shop owners, as well as builders, taxidermists, electricians and anyone within 50 miles who could understand her creative visions and would assist in bringing her weird and wonderful projects to life. I never knew who or what would be in the house when I got home from school. One day it might be our electrician friend, Dave, sitting in the kitchen wearing a pink wig, playing an electric guitar and laughing with my parents. Other days, Mom's spiritual friends would visit, and she'd invite me to sit with them and they would read my animal signs and teach me that happiness was more powerful than hate, and that I must harness this energy. They would talk about the energetic portals in their closets and what came through these portals and how they were dealing with the bedroom traffic they caused.

My mom also introduced me to a list of books and seminar tapes. I read every kind of self-help, spirituality, and consciousness book she had and bought many more of my own, doing all of the exercises within them. I read tarot cards for hours a day, gave serious thought to subscribing to a specific religion, and I worked hard to harness the power of my subconscious mind.

I loved learning and had a true lust for knowing everything I could possibly know. I became obsessed with advanced human sociology and metaphysics and anything that might give me more information about the mysteries of the universe.

At eight years of age, I wanted to go to Sunday School. The Children's Picture Bible I had requested for Christmas failed to satiate and I needed to know more about the Christian religion. Although my parents were not religious, they always let me lead my own life, even at such a young age. So, off to Sunday School I went. I flummoxed the Sunday School teacher with my deep religious question: "If God made everything, who made God?" I imagine I must also have looked quite hilarious, being so small yet so existential.

My relentless questioning continued. I remember being twelve years old, gazing intently at the sky thinking, "If Buddhist Monks can have total enlightenment beyond human reality, then what am I going to have to do to get that? Where do I have to go? Who do I have to see? What do I have to read? Please somebody show me." Sometimes I would ask out loud, sometimes quietly in my head. Sooner or later, something or someone would show up with more information about what I was looking for. I was convinced that there had to be at least one person on this planet who had awareness of everything in the world and universe, who could teach me the things I desperately needed to know.

When I was thirteen, I attended a workshop about having a conversation with your body. The room was filled with adults aged forty to sixty. I was on my own, a kid, learning these uncommon techniques and endlessly curious about my body's own consciousness and capacities – what else could it tell me about what was possible in life?

My seeming boundless curiosity and energy in life earned me the nickname of "Tigger" (the "bouncy, pouncy, fun-fun-fun-

fun-fun" tiger from *Winnie the Pooh*) from my mom because I was always jumping around on my tail, excited about everything and anything. A lot of the time, that really was me, and I was my true Tigger self: happy, energetic, curious, and playful.

But as is often the case with creative seekers, the thing that makes us so attuned to the possibilities of life can also make us deeply aware of the not so great. For me, this meant that while the tapestry of life was rich, it was also intense, and I experienced times of deep struggle. Sometimes I could beat it, and other times it was really hard. The first time I remember it being particularly difficult was at age fifteen, when my wonderful Uncle Wayne drowned in the ocean. This changed the structure of our close farm family, and it changed my mental health along with it.

My Uncle Wayne was someone who has seen the unkindness of the world and chose something different. He'd suffered a lot of abuse growing up. He was a big, burly man, yet kind and sweet. He loved his kids, and he loved us, his nieces. He didn't talk a lot, but he was a really cool energy to have around. He and my dad were both farmers, and they did all the farming together. They'd come off the field and eat together every day. I loved it when Uncle Wayne was around, and I would cook. He would say, "If you cook any better, Julia, you are going to have men lined up from here to Burdette Corner," which was a half mile down the road. One time, I got a weird rash on my foot, and he came around with a tube of cream and said, 'This might help.' A seemingly small thing, and yet the kindness it came along with stays with me even now. He gave us money for doing well in school. He made an effort to create a sense of love and caring, to be the kindness he desired in the world, even when he had not always received it himself.

I remember when my Uncle Wayne was turning sixty and I was so excited about his birthday. I was on the school bus going on and on about it to my friend, Katie: "I can't believe my Uncle Wayne is sixty!" We were going to a steak house an hour and a half away in the city, that was reserved for the most special of occasions. It was only a month later that he died. It was unexpected and tragic. This powerful, kind presence that had been so substantial in my world was now gone and a gaping hole remained. My family was profoundly affected, and I found the intensity of the grief, both spoken and unspoken, weighed very heavily.

After Uncle Wayne's death, I would go through deep periods of depression, finding it almost impossible to move from one side of the bed to the other, because it seemed like everything in my body was made of lead. In those times, I felt like the future vanished, and I would never come out of that hell-ridden space.

Over time, my family was healing from the tragedy, yet my mental health still went up and down without warning.

Looking back, I realise that much of the depression and what I believed was my own struggle was actually my extreme capacity of awareness. I didn't yet have the tools that I will share with you later in this book, but I still had my burning curiosity. I would come out of my down episodes, continuing to search for the secret to life, the joy of the universe, and ultimately, the greatness of consciousness.

CHAPTER 2
A New Adventure

When I was eighteen, I left my small town and went to college in Winnipeg. I was eager to do this because I needed new adventures in order to grow. I hoped the change of environment would give me answers at a faster rate. In Winnipeg, there would be far more options to explore.

On my first day of college, my mom and I were getting out of the car when we saw a girl with two big faux-fur pillows getting out of another car. One was yellow and one fuchsia pink. My mom said, "There, Julia, there is your new friend!"

As we walked up, the girl with the pillows went up the elevator and into the same dorm room as me. That was how I met my new best friend and roommate for the next four years, Jessie. Jessie became my new family. Like me, she grew up on a farm. She had also lived all over the world with her parents who were doing incredible projects, mostly in Indonesia, working with farmers in sustainable agriculture. Her parents were radicals and spiritualists, and although Jessie liked athletics and wanted something of a more normal life for herself than her parents had, she was well suited to living with a deep-seeking nut job like me.

In that first year of school, beyond my full course load, I attended radical yoga workshops, sex and S&M workshops, meditation workshops and Zumba dance classes. Jessie and I also had a shared calendar with all the clubs and bars in the city and had strict plans to party at each one of them. Outside of this, I continued to seek deeper meaning.

When I met a man at a yoga workshop who said he had accessed his kundalini energy, I had to know more. When I went to talk to him after the workshop, he was so strung out on drugs, I couldn't make sense of what he was saying. I would have to seek these answers elsewhere.

When I saw a poster for a BDSM workshop (BDSM is a form of sexual role playing, similar to what you see in the movie *50 Shades of Grey*. It stands for Bondage and Discipline, Dominance and Submission, Sadism and Masochism.) I went to the sex shop it was being held in, dressed in a pretty purple flowered shirt, and sat right up front of the arranged chairs, notebook and fluffy pen at the ready to take notes. I must have looked like Reese Witherspoon's character in *Legally Blonde*, where she starts out at Harvard and is a little different and underprepared for the culture and education.

A doctor whose specialty was human sexuality came out, did a sterile talk on sex, and then introduced the small group of attendees to our demonstrators.

"Oh good! A demonstration would help," I thought. I wasn't totally privy regarding what was to come.

A couple wearing combat boots stood up from the back row, came to the front and began. The woman had a shaved head, a black tank top, black leggings, and glasses. The man was wearing black

Army pants and a black tank top, and had many tattoos. For the next hour and a half, I watched, eyes exploding out of my head, as five feet in front of me, they cut each other's clothes off with special knives and whipped each other back and forth lovingly, with different types of flogs and whips. They chained each other up and spanked each other, all the while teaching us the etiquette, safety phrases, and healthy S&M procedures. Putting dog collars on each other, they walked each other around the tiny space at the back of the sex shop, moaning in pleasure with each act they undertook. It was fascinating, hilarious, shocking, intriguing, and probably not a lifestyle I was going to take on.

I ran home to Jessie to tell her what I had just witnessed. We had a good laugh as I described how out of place I must have looked, dressed in my flowery top, and we marveled at the fact that there is such diversity in the world.

I truly enjoyed my first year of university and exploring this new world, and I was still seeking more. Thankfully, it wasn't far around the corner.

CHAPTER 3

Thank Goodness! New Tools for Consciousness

The next year in September was our second year at university. The month after our school year started, I got an excited call from my mom. I was sitting upstairs in the main building of the university, staring out the window and in agony over a quantitative research project, when my little flip phone rang. My mom immediately expounded, "Quick! Check your email. Judy just sent me a link to this amazing radio interview about something called Access Consciousness. It's really good."

Normally I wouldn't stop what I was doing to listen to a radio show, but my mom's enthusiasm and a feeling in my gut pulled me in to listen. It was incredible. The lady was talking about being in line at the deli and craving a ham sandwich. She posed the question, "When you have thoughts like that, is it you who is thinking you want the ham sandwich, or are you psychic and picking up on someone else in line thinking that?" It was a simple example, but as someone who was so often disappointed with things I ordered at the deli, this one question put a whole lot into perspective for me. So much of what I was thinking on a daily basis didn't feel like me, and this was the first time someone acknowledged that I am actually picking up on the thoughts of others.

The woman also spoke about how something that is true for you, makes you feel lighter, and a lie always makes you feel heavier. For example, if you spend a lot of time thinking, "I'm really stupid," and it doesn't feel light when you say or think it, you might acknowledge that it is heavy, and actually not true. Being aware of what is heavy and light is also how you can make choices that work for you.

This whole conversation excited me because I realised that I was being shown how to use my questioning nature with tools like light and heavy to become more aware of what was true for me, and what wasn't. I started using heavy and light to ask my body what food it would like to eat, and what social events and parties to go to. When I was asked out on a date, I would ask myself, "What will this date be like?" and if the energy I sensed was light, I'd go on the date. I had a lot of awesome dates!

Another Access tool I learned is called, "Who does this belong to?™" The challenge I was given was to ask this question for every thought, feeling and emotion I had through the entire day – and keep doing this for at least three days. Each time you ask the question, if the thought, feeling or emotion lightens up at all, even half of a percent, it isn't yours. When you acknowledge it isn't yours, you can also acknowledge that you do not have to act on it or do anything about it, because it was never yours to deal with in the first place.

"Who does this belong to?" is also described as "becoming a walking, talking meditation" because it invites you to acknowledge that you really are so aware that you pick up on everything – and most of it isn't yours! The more I played with this tool, I became clearer and lighter. I didn't feel so burdened with a million thoughts and feelings. It gave me a perspective on the depressive times I'd been struggling with particularly after Uncle Wayne's death. Like the ham sandwich craving that the lady on the radio described, I was aware of other people's thoughts and also their sadness and grief. I had struggled to deal with it all because I was misinterpreting it as my own. As these tools kept reminding me – what is true for you is light. Anything heavy doesn't belong to you. This opened the door to a whole new world of awareness. I found this utterly fascinating, and I knew I wanted more of wherever this was leading me.

The next year I met the founders of Access Consciousness, Gary Douglas and Dr. Dain Heer.

The thing I knew about Gary was that he was living in the world I wanted to live in. I had been searching so hard and for so long, I could tell by the way he looked around the room, by the way he walked and talked that he had what I desired in life. He embodied the energy of consciousness that I was looking for; a true joy in being alive. Gary also has this amazing way of morphing into different energies to match what people need. When I met him, I saw different members of my family in him and felt very much at home.

Dr. Dain Heer's energy was infectious and being around him was so much fun. His classes had this blast of power of a different universe, mixed with the wit and humour of Jim Carrey. Dain is basically a great gift to the world. He has personally empowered healing and change for hundreds of thousands, if not millions of individuals through his kindness, his willingness to be different and to acknowledge the difference in you.

When I was around Gary and Dain, I felt more connected to the universe. I was at peace. I was finally getting somewhere in my quest to embody the ecstasy of being alive. I started going to Access classes and I would occasionally skip a few days of school and travel to Toronto or Vancouver, even as far as Rome and Costa Rica to attend classes with Gary and Dain and continue my journey into consciousness.

Gary and Dain also spoke very differently about energy. Energy is not good or bad or negative or positive. Energy is not a finite resource – it is unlimited. Energy is also our first language. When you come into this world as a baby, you are using the language of energy. You know how to cry at a certain pitch to get your parents' attention. The ability to do that requires energetic awareness. We do it naturally, then we start learning from people around us about how to think and use judgement instead. And boy, is life and growing up all about learning how to judge!

Gary and Dain are very clever, because light and heavy is a beginner tool for teaching you to re-connect with your innate awareness of energy and to choose based on the energy of things, rather than trying to get it right from a logical or rational point of view. Logical and linear thinking actually limits what you can create. When you are using your awareness of energy to choose what will expand your life, you might make choices that do not make sense to anyone else, but they will tend to work out greater than you can imagine. When you begin to trust your sense of heavy and light – your awareness of energy – and you play with it, it is the beginning of a magical way of living.

CHAPTER 4

Creating with Energy

While the concept of energy is often considered esoteric, I believe it should be considered mainstream, because it is part of who and what we are. It is also highly pragmatic.

The energy pull tool that I dedicate the majority of this book to is one of the most simple and versatile ways to play with energy and create more in life.

An energy pull is an exercise in which you ask the energy of the universe to contribute to what you are creating. When you ask the universe to contribute, it means you are engaging with and being supported by the molecules of every plant, animal, and being in the world and the universe. The universe desires to support you. Consciousness desires to support you. The earth itself desires to support you. EVERYTHING desires to support you. Each molecule has consciousness and when you ask the molecules to rearrange themselves, they will. You just have to be willing to let it in.

Using energy to create may look to others like you have superpowers, but what you are doing is using your awareness to guide things in a direction that makes problems and pain fall to the background and joy come to the forefront. Energy is quick, simple and dynamic. It's easy. Most people are used to having it hard, and think if something is too easy, there must be a catch.

I'll admit that allowing things to come to you more easily can feel really weird at first. One of the most difficult parts about consciousness and energy for me, was learning that doing what works doesn't have a rationale or logic that makes sense to my mind, or anyone else's. Being such a serious searcher from a young age, I was always trying to figure things out with my head. Once I stopped trying to understand cognitively and allowed myself to play with energy with no thought and no point of view, that's when things really changed for me.

I had heard about all the amazing things Gary had helped other people do, and I really desired a one-on-one session with him. At the time, Gary was doing sessions in person, in Denver, Colorado so I booked a time and went to see him. I was twenty years old and so excited! Gary was so sweet, so lovely, so... something indescribable. But one thing was for sure – he could see right through me.

I told Gary all the things I wanted to create in my life. I wanted to have a successful business facilitating consciousness, but I was very young and worried my business may be too weird for people to be interested in exploring. Many people thought I was strange for doing something like Access Consciousness. They thought I should be doing something more normal, something they could understand.

Yet, here I was, doing something incomprehensible in a city where nobody used the tools of Access Consciousness. Basically, I was all alone, so I asked Gary how I could create a thriving business and how I could share the tools with other people.

He described the simple process of doing an energy pull for my business and said, "You need to do the energy pull every day for 90 days."

Gary also invited me to ask this question: *"Universe, who can you send me today to keep me on my way?"* I did exactly as he suggested, and almost right away, all kinds of things came into my life!

After starting my 90 days of energy pulls, people were finding me from all over the place. I ended up renting a room in a converted mansion at a place called the University Women's Club. It had an annual membership fee of $650 which let me use the house whenever I wanted to do sessions and classes with people. I was the only member under seventy years of age. The club was old-fashioned and proper and was such a beautiful space that it made everything I did there more fun. There was even a bald butler who took care of us and brought us snacks! I used to set up a room full of massage tables on a weekly basis to do Access Consciousness Bars[1] trades there. It became a hub where people could find me and the tools.

People from all walks of life found me there. There were people who rode Harley Davidson motorcycles. One woman was a prison guard. Somebody else was a medical doctor. Another was an x-ray technician. I had retired women coming to me, and a man who was an English teacher and theater teacher. One lady was a real estate agent and had what I considered a second career being a crazy cat lady. These people became my friends.

---

[1] Access Bars® was developed by Gary. It is a gentle, hands-on technique that involves touching specific points on the head, helping quiet the mind and promote relaxation.

The people who showed up were the weirdos of society, and we all lived in freezing cold Winnipeg. We had so much fun with each other and learned so much from each other. And here I was, their little twenty-year-old facilitator.

My classes kept growing and in the often minus twenty-five degree celcius winter in Winnipeg, you could find me lugging massage tables at 7 a.m. by myself from the boot of the Chevy Impala my dad had given me into the old, converted mansion. I loved running around getting the snacks, going back and forth to Staples to have manuals printed, and doing anything I could to set the scene for these classes.

I became an infectious energy of possibility and everything and everyone that could contribute to that came out of the woodwork to be a part of it.

Around the time I graduated from university, I suddenly felt the desire to expand my life and business beyond Winnipeg to something different and unfamiliar. I wondered what else was possible for me and I started creating new adventures for myself. I'll share more about that in later chapters, but for now, let's explore the essential elements of the energy pull and how to do them.

PART TWO

CHAPTER 5

Exploring the Energy Pull

One of the laws of the universe is *ask and you will receive*. Energy pulls are a dynamic way of asking the universe for what you would like to have in your life. The more energies you are willing to include, the more magic you can create. The more you put your mind aside and play with the undefined energy of things, the more you will invite possibilities that exist beyond the limits of your mind. When you pull energy, you are including the universe in everything you create. That is a lot of contribution coming toward you.

If you think that you don't understand exactly how to pull energy at first, that is not a problem. In truth, you have been moving energy your whole life, you just haven't acknowledged that's what you were doing. For example, have you ever thought to yourself, "It would be nice if I had this thing in my life," forgot about it, then a few days later, it showed up, seemingly out of nowhere? That's you being an energy of the "ask" and receiving it when it showed up. Like I said earlier, energy really is simple. You are the maestro that can use it in all kinds of ways you haven't yet explored.

A crucial step in claiming your energetic capacities is to become aware of how the energy you choose to *be* in life generates everything that shows up – the good and the bad. You are the source for the energies that create your life, so it helps if you are willing to become aware of when you are using energy *for* you, and *against* you. When you realise that the energy *you choose* is what creates your life, you can change the energy that's creating what you don't desire, and play more with the energies that will create more of what you do desire.

Would you like to become more in tune with your abilities with energy from now on? If so, great! In the next few chapters, I am going to break down the elements of the energy pull and show you how to start using them.

And, as I've mentioned before, there really is no right or wrong way to do any of this. Energy isn't right or wrong. You are not right or wrong. Please, don't judge you, and please have fun with this!

THE ENERGY PULL ELEMENTS

The first thing you need to know about the elements of doing an energy pull, is that they are all easy. It may initially be a challenge to get your logical mind out of the way. But once you have more ease with that (and I'll keep giving you tips and reminders to help you along), you'll appreciate the elegance of this process. It truly requires no thinking, no effort – just relax and play.

An energy pull is broken down into a few steps:

1. Relax.
2. Expand your energy.

3. Perceive the energy of what you would like to ask for.

4. Put that energy out in front of your body. I'll refer to this as putting the energy into an "energy bubble" in front of you, but you don't have to visualise a bubble for it to work.

5. Pull energy from the whole universe into that energy bubble until your heart/chest warms up or expands.

6. Send out trickles of that energy back into the universe so that all the people, things, and possibilities that match the energy of what you are asking for know where to find you.

Six simple steps, that is it! If you are already getting a sense of how easy this is, that's fantastic. And if you are scratching your head and thinking, "What does she mean by 'expand your energy' exactly?" – fear not – because we are going to dive into all of that right now.

CHAPTER 6

Steps 1 & 2: Relax and Expand Your Energy

Are you an infinite being or a finite being?

From the time I was very small, I had a sense of being part of something larger, of being able to perceive beyond where my body was in physical space. I didn't really have words for this sense until, as a young adult, I was asked the question, "Are you a finite being inside a body, or an infinite being with a body inside of it?"

The energy of "infinite being with a body" created such an expansive sense of relaxation and lightness for me, it felt as though my body was saying, "Finally, you've acknowledged what is true for both of us!"

The idea that you are a spacious, limitless being that encompasses your body and far beyond it, might be something you've never considered before. Have you spent your life assuming that you and your body are the same thing? Or that you are just a little mind or soul inside of a body? What if your soul, being, essence – whatever you choose to call it – does not have outside edges?

Take a moment now to ask yourself, "Am I an infinite being, or a finite being?" If you try to find the edges of your being, can you find them? Or does it seem more like wherever you expand your awareness, that's where you are?

Which feels lighter to you and your body – finite or infinite? Remember, what is light for you, is true.

The reason I invite you to play with the sense of you as an infinite being, is that every energy pull in this book starts with a fundamental practice: relaxing and expanding your energy far beyond your body. When you allow your energy to expand, you encompass more space.

Why would you desire to have more space? Space allows new possibilities. Space is also what nature is. Have you ever walked in nature and felt more relaxed and at peace, the tension easing from your body and mind? We've all experienced moments of having a greater sense of space, where we've allowed ourselves to "decompress". What if you could consciously choose to be more space instantaneously, anytime and anywhere?

Being spacious and joyful and at ease is more true for us than anything else. Unfortunately, we grow up learning many ways to eliminate our sense of space. Anytime you believe you are limited or incapable, or you focus on pain or problems, you compress yourself down from infinite being into finite being and eliminate the space you actually are.

You can only have a problem or a difficulty when you're not receiving the contribution that's available and when you assume you are a small, finite being, rather than an infinite one.

Expanding your energy is an act of acknowledging and embodying your connectedness to the universe. More than that, it's allowing yourself to be part of the universe, rather than trying to maintain this idea that you are a separate, powerless thing confined to your limited existence.

ENERGY EXPANSION EXERCISE

STEP 1. RELAX.

- Sit or lie down. Close your eyes or soften your focus. Put your attention on your body. Where are you relaxed? Where are you tense? Are there spots in your body you are noticing for the first time in a while? Say hello to them and invite them to relax. You might even enjoy just resting and breathing in and out slowly for a couple of minutes. Give your body the time and space to slowly melt the tension and relax more and more.
- Notice your feet on the floor or your body on the mattress or sofa. Place your hands on your stomach and feel the sensation of your hands on your stomach, and your stomach on your hands as you breathe. Notice the top of your head, and the bottom of your feet.

STEP 2. EXPAND.

- Perceive the space that is just outside of your skin, like where the little hairs on your arms are.
- From the space just beyond the outside of your skin, expand your attention further out, to the size of the room that you're in, and expand to the top four corners of the

room that you are in. Then expand out to the bottom four corners of the room. Notice that wherever you put your attention, there you are. You are so much bigger than just your physical body!

- Now, expand your energy out over the whole building you are in. Expand out over the city block, street or road, and far out over the city or town.
- At this point, your mind may not be able to keep track. That's great. Let go. Keep relaxing. Don't try to visualise or focus, just allow yourself to have the "sense" of your energy expanding further.
- Continue to expand your energy outwards until you reach the oceans, then expand beyond your country, beyond your continent, over the entire world until you fill the atmosphere and go down to the core of the earth. Keep expanding your energy out in all directions.

STEP 3. RELAX MORE. EXPAND MORE.

- Check in with your body. Notice any changes in the senses going on in your body. Are you more relaxed? Are you breathing more easily? Nothing you are perceiving or experiencing is right or wrong. Just notice your body and how it feels right now.
- Now, from wherever you are, ask for more expansion: go beyond the outer atmosphere. Go beyond the solar system, beyond each planet, beyond our galaxy. Expand your energy out into the farthest reaches of the universe,

as far as you can possibly go. And when you come to an end of where you think you can expand, what if you would expand just a little bit further beyond it?

- REMEMBER: If you are asking to expand out, you are doing it. You may experience some different sensations, or you may feel nothing at all. It may feel just like your body relaxing and some tension releasing. You may sense it like a little more space between your molecules, feeling less heavy or solid. Or maybe you'll feel more weighty as your body finally relaxes and lets your tight muscles go. Notice whatever sensations occur and keep asking for your energy to expand. If at any time you start tensing, efforting, or trying too hard, just notice it and then allow yourself to relax and let go.

- Enjoy the sense of expansion for a couple more minutes. Then, before you get up and go about your day, just notice any difference in your energy and your body from when you started. Has anything changed? Do you feel any lighter? Happier? More calm? If you like, why not sit or lay there and indulge in the space and expansion a little longer?

Now that you've experienced what it is like when you expand your energy, what would it be like if you allowed yourself to be at least this spacious from now on? What more magic and possibilities can you invite when you are willing to be a space as big as the universe?

CHAPTER 7

Step 3: Requesting with Energy

The energy you put your attention on is what gets created in your life. Energy pulls invite you to be present and aware of the energy you are choosing each moment, and to pull more of what you desire into your life. Have you noticed that the times you are happier and laughing more, life tends to flow with more ease? And conversely, when you are upset or problem-focused, more upset and problems seem to spring up? Did you visualise that into being? Or was it your energy – the attitudes you embodied – that allowed your enjoyment (or suffering) in life to show up?

Many manifestation techniques will teach you about visualisation – getting the picture of what you'd like your life to look like in order to have it. I used to spend hours visualising things and then getting frustrated when they didn't manifest. What I now know is that visualisation narrows down what the universe can gift to you to such a miniscule size, you are literally stopping the universe from contributing to you in all the magical ways it desires to. Perceiving and requesting with energy is quicker and easier than picturing it, and is a method that matches you as an infinite being far more than visualisation.

Let me give you an example of the difference between requesting with energy versus visualisation:

If you would like to get a car, and you ask for a car that is fun to drive and brings you joy every time you get in it, the universe can easily contribute to you creating that. With that request, you are showing the universe the energy – the joy and fun of driving a car you love – and are willing to receive a car that will create that energy in your life. If you ask from a specific image of, say, a white BMW, the universe cannot contribute to that as easily. If you have decided you only desire a white BMW, and there is actually a greater possibility for you, but you are stuck on that white BMW as the only choice, then the universe can't bring you anything, because you're not willing to receive something greater, because you'll reject anything and everything that isn't a white BMW. The universe cannot give you what you are unwilling to receive.

What I am saying is that visualisation is a more cumbersome method than perceiving energy. It's harder work, because visualisation means you have to stop the flow of energy to focus on one point. When you request of the universe based on the energetic sense of what you'd like your life to *be* like (rather than look like), it opens the door to broader possibility, leaving more energetic flow and space, which is how the universe actually functions.

And, if like me, you have continually failed at using visualisation methods to bring things into your life, energy pulls may be more suited to you. When you use energy as the tool of request, many, many things that match that energy can show up, and often with more speed, ease and abundance.

Rather than trying to visualise your future, you want to perceive energies that are congruent with your being and invite them to come into your life in all the magical and infinite ways that the universe can possibly provide.

ENERGY REQUEST EXERCISE

STEP 1. What makes you and your body feel light and joyful?

- What do you love to do that makes you and your body happy to be alive? Can you recall the sense it gives your body? For me, I love nautical and ocean energies. When I see yachts in the harbor, and feel the sunlight as the ocean glistens around me, it contributes a sense of peace and beauty to my soul. I also love spending time in the kitchen. From buying ingredients at the local markets, to simmering delicious cuisines on the stove, it's a total delight.
- Spend a couple of minutes recalling what it is like for you and your body when you do something joyful for you. While you are perceiving those energies, ask, "*What would it take for that energy to show up for me even more?*" That is the beginning of requesting with energy.

STEP 2. What energies would nurture your life?

- Are there energies that you would like more of in your life because they create a sense of peace and ease? For example, would you like to feel more nurtured in your life? Would you like a greater sense of joy and relaxation with everything you do? What energies could contribute to your life? Nurturing touch is something that's very important to me. I wanted to have more of it in my life, so I pulled energy to receive more touch, having no idea how it would show up. Shortly after asking for this, I met my now husband- Anthony, who has an incredible amount of nurturance and care in his world and his touch. But what I didn't expect was his three kids, who became my step-kids. They loved to cuddle and so the nurturing energy in my world exponentialised even more. It did not show up at all the way I thought it would!

- Indulge for a few minutes in the energies that you'd like more of and what it would be like to have them in your life, substantially, every day. Then ask: *What are the infinite ways these energies can show up in my life?*

There is no right or wrong energy to ask for. Even though I'm inviting you to play with energy rather than try to visualise what you want – you can still ask for specific things, too. Ask for a white BMW, ask for a house, or a million dollars. You can ask for anything. All I suggest is that as you ask, you leave the door open for even more to come to you.

I used the energy pulls to ask for these three kind of "specific" things:

1. To live near the ocean, in a warm climate, in a place that was nurturing to my body.

2. To live in a beautiful, white, southern-style house (like in *The Notebook* movie!), and

3. To be surrounded by amazing people who were as interested in consciousness as I was and were happy for me when I changed.

These were "tangible" things, but I still connected with the energetic sense of what that would be like, living in my beautiful house, living by the ocean, of my body being constantly nurtured, and the sense of being surrounded by amazing people who celebrated my change and success alongside me. I had my dreams, but I was also open to the infinite possibilities of what that could look like and how it could show up, that might be very different to any specific images I had.

CHAPTER 8

Steps 4 - 7: Pulling & Trickling Energy

As I mentioned back in Chapter Five, you and your body already know how to move and flow energy, you just might not have called it that. For example, have you ever dealt with a pushy salesman and had that immediate reaction of desiring to pull away? That is your awareness of someone pushing a lot of energy at you. Have you ever spent time with a cute baby or young kid that you just couldn't stop cuddling or gushing over – or a puppy or a kitten? That irresistible pull is them pulling energy. Have you ever felt tired and depleted, then someone gave you a warm hug that made you feel relaxed and energised after? That's receiving a flow of energy toward you. Pulling energy is just directing flows of energy in the direction you ask.

Energy is also an infinite resource. It doesn't run out and it can't run out. If you ask for more energy, it will show up. You can move it, flow it, push it, pull it, increase it, decrease it. You can expand it, compress it, and of course, you can create what you desire with it. What would it be like for you to create your life from now on, knowing that you have infinite energetic resources, with truly no limit? Eek! Is it just me, or are you getting a little excited about what is possible for you?

Now it is time for enjoying the final steps of the energy pull:

STEP 4. Putting the energy in front of you in an "energy bubble",

STEP 5. Pulling energy into the energy bubble, and

STEP 6. Sending trickles back out to all the places in the universe where those energies exist so they know where to find you.

STEP 7. Reversing the flow, and again, pulling energy through the universe, through the bubble, through our body, and out the back of your body into the universe.

If you are wondering exactly "how" to pull the energy or trickle the energy in this part of the process, I'll give you the secret: just ask. Just like when you were expanding your energy in earlier chapters, it starts with a request. If you are having any trouble with this idea, just think of it as being the same as asking someone to pass you the salt at dinner. You ask, and you may not know exactly how or via whom it'll come to you, but you're not even really thinking about it, you just know it's definitely coming.

Let's put all the steps together and I'll walk you through a complete energy pull.

ENERGY PULL EXERCISE

- Relax and expand your energy, continuing out to the whole universe.
- Perceive the energies you'd like to invite into your life. You can use any of the energies you played with in Chapter

Seven, or you can simply ask for something like, "I'd like more joy," or, "I'd like to laugh more."

- Put that energy in front of you, into the energy bubble.
- *Now, you are going to pull through the energy bubble from all over the universe. Just ask the energy to pull.* You can literally say in your head or out loud, "Energy, pull please," or "Okay, I'm pulling energy now" or just "Pull". You can do it without words too, as a completely energetic request. Whichever way you choose to do it, just know that you are now pulling energy. You may have a sense of energy flowing through you and your body, and you may feel nothing. That's totally okay.
- *Pull energy through the whole universe, through that bubble of energy in front of you, and through your entire body and out the back of you.* Pull energy through every pore of your body and being, let it be big and expansive. If it helps, imagine you are pulling big rivers of easy, rushing energy, from all directions, from everywhere.
- *Keep pulling until you have a sense of your heart area opening or warming up.* This is your "indicator" that you've opened up to the energy of the universe and have now created space to receive.
- *Reverse the flow slightly and let little trickles of energy go out to all of the things, beings and possibilities that will contribute to creating your phenomenal life.* Sending those trickles out creates an energetic connection, so all those people and things will know how to find you.

- Then to finish, you reverse the flow so you are pulling energy again. Do one big final pull and let the energy wash through the universe, through the bubble, through your body and out the back of your body, into the universe.
- And that's it – you have now completed one full energy pull!

How was that for you? Was it something completely new and different? Or did the energy pull, or parts of it, remind you of something you actually already do and be? As I've now mentioned probably a couple of times – energy is totally natural to you. IT is what you are and what you can choose to create with. Now that you've acknowledged it more openly and become more present with energy, what magic can you now create?

PART THREE
THE ENERGY PULLS

CHAPTER 9
Hedonism

Are you willing to ask for the pleasure, joy and sweetness that is possible in life?

If so, you may be a *hedonist!* I'll take a minute to explain what hedonism truly is, because there are some mistaken assumptions that often fly alongside it, discouraging us from looking at the gift it is.

The origin of the word *hedonism* comes from the Greek words *hēdonē*, meaning *pleasure*, and its close relative *hēdys*, meaning *sweet*. There was also a branch of philosophy or doctrine based on hedonism, which explored the idea that the chief goal in life is happiness and pleasure. In other words, "What if the purpose of life was to have fun?"

If you ask me, there isn't anything bad about that at all, unless having fun and enjoying your life is terrible, bad and wrong. Actually, I'm pretty sure you all know a few people who react as if something is wrong with you when you are "too" happy. But, let's forget those people for the moment and get back to the fun stuff...

In its pure form, without judgement attached, a hedonist is *one who seeks the pleasure, joy and sweetness of life*. It is only modern-day usage that has included a negative connotation, implying that hedonists typically derive pleasure from overly self-indulgent or debaucherous pursuits; specifically, the *really* fun stuff that people judge the most.

Have you bought into that assumption at all? If someone called you a hedonist, would you be flattered or offended? Would you say, "Oh yes, that's me, I'm all about the pleasure I can have in life!" or would you think, "I beg your pardon? Are you calling me selfish?" How much have you avoided pursuing the immense pleasure of your life just because you don't want to be judged?

When you buy into judgements about hedonism, you avoid the gift that hedonism is. That is something I'd really like to change, because I think we all deserve to have as much pleasure in living as we choose!

What if hedonism – the pleasure and sweetness that is truly available to you – was part of everything you create from now on? What would that be like?

In the following exercise and energy pull, I'm going to ask you about what you truly desire in life. Please include the energy of hedonism in this. When you add the willingness to have joy, sweetness and pleasure in every part of your life, the universe can gift you much, much more.

EXERCISE: WHAT DO YOU TRULY DESIRE?

To create a life that really works for you, you must be willing to invite and engage with energies that are congruent with you and what you truly desire – not just the energies that you've been taught to believe you should choose and which are supposed to be fulfilled by getting the partner, the 2.5 kids, the job, the dog, and the white picket fence. That is why I started this chapter with the energy of hedonism, because it opens the door for you to look at the degree of magic that you are and that goes far beyond what is deemed appropriate or desirable by those around you.

It can feel like a bit of a stretch to connect to these energies at first, because you've been entrained to so many external ideas of what happiness, success and joy should and could be for you.

You have to start from a place of wonder, asking what you truly desire in your life beyond what you've considered before. Then, be willing to have an adventure instead of going into all the usual ideas about what a desirable life is. As you do these energy pulls, *ask the universe to show you what matches the energy of you, the being*, and stay curious and open. You'll become more aware of what is congruent with your true desires. As we go deeper into the chapters of this book, I'll also give you more tools for having clarity around what you'd like to choose. So, please come back to this exercise and energy pull again and again as you discover more of what you'd like to create and add to your life.

For now, let's get started with two things to do every day to guide you on your way:

1. Ask yourself, *"What do I truly desire?"* with regards to your life. You can pick one area of your life to ask this about, or just ask it as a general, "whole life" question - there's no right or wrong! Use this question as an open-ended exercise. The question is your invitation to the universe. You are opening an energetic door to possibilities, and

allowing things to come to you in their own time, while you get on with living.

2. I'm going to emphasise an essential element of the exercise: every time you ask yourself "What do I truly desire?" do not try to answer it or predict anything. Do not try to figure it out, picture it or decide what has to show up. If you catch yourself trying to do any of these things, *stop, relax, let go of control or fixation on the outcome,* and ask the universe to show you: *"Universe, please show me what I desire and all the myriad of ways it can show up for me."*

The universe is going to be able to manifest your desires far easier and more abundantly than your brain can. It will respond to your question by bringing a multitude of possibilities into your life. These possibilities may show up in a day, a month, or a year. The universe does not function from time, so if you are fixed on what and when, you make it harder for the universe to gift to you. Let go and allow the universe to contribute to you. Your job is to ask, to relax, and be open to receiving all the miraculous ways your desires can show up that you've never even considered.

I'm going to add a third item to this list:

3. Trust you. Trust the universe. Don't get stuck on figuring out what the next step or next "right" choice is that you have to make in order to have what you desire. Instead, be willing to choose anything and know you can't mess it up. Sometimes the fastest way to discover what you desire is by discovering what you do not.

A great example of where I allowed myself to choose what didn't work, until I discovered what did, was with dating and relationships. I used to choose guys to date because they were popular or had a sort of social power. I thought if I could get them, it meant that I was also powerful or gaining some kind of strength. As I became more aware of what my choices were creating, I realised that choosing from judgement was not creating what I wanted. I had decided I needed an external energy of "power" to be more powerful myself. I was picking guys who created more judgement in my world rather than men who were kind, caring and nurturing, which was more congruent with the energy I actually desired in life. I'm grateful for all my dating and relationship choices, because every time I chose, I gained more awareness. As my awareness grew, I became more willing to recognise both the energies I truly desired, and the kind of men I could choose that would contribute to that.

So, to recap quickly:

1. Be in question and don't try to figure it all out.

2. Allow the universe to show you possibilities in its own time.

3. Trust you. Be willing to choose anything as you go forward and don't worry about getting it wrong, because every choice will give you more awareness.

With that in mind, let's begin pulling in more of what you truly desire!

ENERGY PULL #1: WHAT DO YOU TRULY DESIRE?

1. Close your eyes and get the sense of your body in the space around you. Relax and expand your energy out to the whole universe. Expand out, just as we practiced earlier in the book, until your energy fills the room. Keep expanding out beyond your city or town, your country, the planet, and out into the universe. Don't try to keep track with your mind. Expand your energy further, increasing the relaxation and sense of space between the molecules of your body.

2. Perceive the energies you'd like to invite into your life. Ask:

    - *What do I truly desire to be, do, have, create and generate in my life?* (and remember: just be with whatever energy is there, don't try to come to an answer in your mind). If you can't get a sense of anything, don't worry! You're doing it, you just may not be feeling anything yet.

    - *Universe, please show me what I desire and all the ways it can show up for me.* Be willing to receive. If you feel any energetic barriers or thoughts and doubts, just imagine pushing them down. Ask the universe to contribute to you having all of this show up with ease. Indulge in the energy of feeling totally supported and facilitated by the universe in having everything you desire, no matter what it may be.

    - *Universe, show me what pleasure and sweetness is available that would make my life so joyful that I barely recognise myself!* Imagine being so relaxed and exuberant in life that you don't even remember why you ever thought you had a problem. How awesome would that be?

3. Put all those energies in front of you, into the energy bubble. Again, don't worry if it "feels" like nothing, just put whatever sense of energy you perceive (even if it's empty air) in front of you.

4. Now, pull energy through the energy bubble, inviting all of your desires to show up with ease. Pull energy through the whole universe from that big, expanded space of your being. Keep pulling just like you're pulling a big river of energy into and through the bubble, then through you, through every cell of your body, and out the back of you.

5. Pull harder, not with more force, but with demand, pulling until you have a sense of your chest or heart area opening.

6. Once you have that sensation, reverse the flow and let little trickles of energy go out to all of the beings and elements that will contribute to creating all of your desires. Relax, and keep trickling it out to all of those things and people so they know where to find you.

7. And finally, reverse the flow and pull again, through the bubble, through you and your body. Pull through the whole universe, through the bubble and through you. Be willing to receive all that energy from the universe. Let your chest, your stomach, your shoulders, and your knees be vulnerable. Vulnerability is the courage to receive all the gifts of the universe without barriers or limits. It can feel exposed and intense and unfamiliar, but it is also glorious.

8. Receive everything the universe so greatly desires to contribute to you every day. By becoming vulnerable, with your barriers down, you are now letting the universe know, "I'm willing to receive more." How much more contribution from the universe can you allow yourself to receive each time you do an energy pull?

And with that, your energy pull is done. The energy will keep going out into the universe to create for you, so relax and enjoy, knowing that you have started a flow of energy into your life that will only get greater the more you choose to engage with it.

Now that you've opened the door to more pleasure and abundance of living, let's dive into a topic I believe we can all create a lot more pleasure with: money!

CHAPTER 10
Money

I grew up in a close-knit community of multi-generational farmers and businesses. My own family had a long local history in the area, and my mom, with great passion, would regale us with the story of our heritage:

Our ancestors were poor Ukrainian immigrants who came to Canada looking for a new opportunity and a new land. In this dead of winter place, they broke the ground – the hard, snowy plains – with their bare hands.

It was really, really bad.

And really, really hard.

Also, they had no food and were starving.

This tale of survival through crushing poverty and hardship was probably meant to instill in my generation an admiration for the hardiness and determination of my ancestors. While I was certainly impressed that they didn't just give up and die under such terrible conditions, my main thought regarding the story was, "No, thank you!" Creating my life through poverty and struggle was something I knew I wasn't going to do.

And then, of course, there was Baba Florence. My maternal grandmother: extravagant, flamboyant, generous, with a voracious penchant for polka music. One look at Baba Florence and it was obvious the memo of our poor Ukrainian heritage had not hit home for her at all. She had money and she *spent* it. She never wore the same outfit twice and had ten closets in her house, all full of clothes. Baba kept *Gloria Gayle's* – the local, yet flashy, women's clothing store – personally in business. Baba Florence was a woman of joyous excess and extreme abundance. She and my grandfather had owned a successful real estate brokerage that bought and sold farmland. Whether she had $5 to her name on any given month, or had just put through a sale for a mutli-million dollar farm, it didn't matter. She was Baba.

She drove a huge, white Lincoln town car that boasted a burgundy velvet interior and a cassette player (because it was the 1990s!) in which she'd play her favourite polka tapes at top volume. She would jump in her seat while she drove and go, "Yip-pee!" At one point, a cassette got stuck in the player and from that day on, all that Lincoln Towncar played was the same side of that same polka cassette. Baba Florence didn't care. She'd come screaming down the road with the windows down, eating handfuls of peanuts as she drove way too fast, bouncing up and down to the polka tunes blasting through her stereo. My sister and I would hear that music as she turned the corner towards our yard, and we'd run to meet her, knowing we were in for a treat!

The trunk of her car was incredibly large, yet she'd stuff it to the brim with all kinds of gifts for us: KFC for our Dad, and all the candy, chips and soda my sister and I loved. We knew she'd have picked up the latest Mary Kate and Ashley VHS at Walmart (her town of 10,000 had a Walmart while our town was much too small). She'd bring coolers filled with whole chickens and vegetables that she grew in her enormous garden plot on the outskirts of town. She'd bring vats of raw honey, and jars of all kinds of foods she'd canned and pickled herself.

At Christmas time, my sister and I were allowed to sleep in the living room by the Christmas tree with Baba. We would pull out the sofa bed portion of the sectional and all cuddle up, admiring the way the light of the full moon glistened on the snow, thinking about how Santa was to come. At around 10 p.m. in the dark of night, Baba Florence would bash something around to make a noise and exclaim, "Listen girls! That's Santa! That's Santa! He's on the roof!"

Baba Florence was an exuberant force in the world. She was also a bit of an anomaly. For most of the people in my family and community, it was much more common to hide abundance and make sure you didn't flaunt any wealth. And you'd never do anything considered too lavish with the money you painstakingly earned. That was considered rude to your neighbours.

While the energy pulls I learned showed me how easily I could generate a business and money, there were many times I'd experience a sense of dissonance between what I knew was possible and the struggle mentality that had been common in my community. I'd start to feel as if I was being abusive to those around me if I allowed myself to have things come to me easily, and then create some money need or problem just to feel that familiar stress and difficulty.

Nowadays, when I catch myself creating struggles with money and get tired of limiting myself, I make a greater choice. That's often when my family will say, "Julia is just like Baba Florence." I'm known for making leaps towards abundance that can be nonsensical to others. In truth, I'd rather make the demand of myself to step up and create more money and more possibilities in my life, than stop my constant shopping, traveling and gifting.

Changing your energy with money can be very uncomfortable at times. Other people won't necessarily understand it. But if I learned anything from Baba Florence and from the energy pulls, it is, "What you choose, you can have". If there were no limit, just joyful possibilities for more, what would you choose?

Let's take some space now to look at the beliefs and ideas around money you've hooked up with, and see what else is possible.

WHAT EDUCATION DID YOU RECEIVE AROUND MONEY?

Money and wealth are some of the most judgeable things on the planet. Every single person on earth grows up being taught limiting and conflicting views, beliefs, and "rights and wrongs" about money. Some spoken, and some unspoken, they all have an energetic component that holds them in place. Unless you take conscious steps to question these energies and explore beyond them, you'll very likely create a financial world similar to your family or community, with some slight variation on the theme.

And so, as I started to look at what I desired my future to be, I had to ask myself: what limitations had I learned around money, and if I didn't buy into them, would that allow me to create something different, fun, and really expansive?

EXERCISE: WHAT'S YOUR MONETARY REALITY?

Take a moment right now to connect energetically with your monetary and financial world.

What comes up for you? It might be a sense of discomfort, stress, or even a strong resistance to getting energetically intimate with your financial reality. Or maybe it is excitement as you sense a new way to play with your finances and money to create something greater. Whatever emerges, relax and be with these energies with as much vulnerability and kindness for you as possible. Nothing will get worse for you by giving this your attention. In fact, quite the opposite. As you look at the energies and ideas you have around money, you can begin to separate out what you learned or picked up that isn't working for you, from what is actually true for you and will work for you.

Grab your favourite note-taking method, and spend a few minutes playing with the energies of your monetary world, writing down whatever comes up as you ask these questions:

When you think of money, deal with money or handle money, what are the instant thoughts, feelings and emotions that come up for you?

Positive or negative, write it all down. Once you have a good list, read them over again.

As you look at each point of view, ask yourself: *"Who does this truly belong to? Where and from whom did I learn these perspectives, feelings, and beliefs about money?"*

You might notice that just about none of what you've written down is just something you've come up with on your own. You picked them up or chose those viewpoints based on someone or something else.

After you've questioned all the items on your list, ask yourself: *"If none of these were real and they all disappeared today, what would I choose my monetary reality to be?"*

NEW ENERGIES FOR YOUR MONEY REALITY

Treading an unfamiliar path doesn't just bring up "stuff" for you. When I started creating my life and business in a really different way, some people in my life were excited and happy for me, while others became concerned or skeptical. When you change, others who've seen you a certain way for a long time can become very uncomfortable. And because we tend to care about the people in our lives, it can be a seductive pull to climb back into those old energies and comfort zones to join them.

For me, experiencing this reaffirmed my desire to more fully examine my "energetic pantry" around money. The old items were still taking up space on the shelves, well past their expiry dates, but I was still hanging on. I needed to continue clearing out the old, and then choose some new energies as my staple items – energies that would facilitate having the monetary reality I truly desired.

ENERGY PULL #2: EASE, PEACE & ENJOYMENT WITH MONEY

The limiting points of view you hold onto about money create barriers to receiving money. For example, if you associate anxious or depressive energies with money, no wonder you are keeping money at an arm's length. However, money and those energies do not have to go together. What if now, you can consciously invite other energies into your relationship with money – ones that will make both you and money happier to hang out and create more together?

I had learned to associate a whole bunch of different energies with money, so when I started to create from a different space, it felt strange. Rather than avoid the discomfort, I became more determined to discover what it would be like to have a truly different relationship with money.

I began that wider exploration with these questions (and I invite you to ask them now, too):

What would it be like to have ease with money?

What would it be like to have a sense of peace with money?

What would it be like to truly enjoy money?

Notice the three key words I mentioned – *Ease. Peace. Joy.*

Have you ever asked that these energies be part of your monetary world?

Take a minute right now to immerse yourself in the sense of what it would be like for you to wake up each day with a deep sense of ease, peace and joy with money. What if every time you thought of money, dealt with finances, or handled money, your sense of ease, peace and joy increased?

As you ask these questions and allow yourself to indulge in what it would be like for you to live each day this way, let's begin an energy pull:

1. Get your body comfortable as you relax and breathe... expand your energy out. Once you are familiar with the energy pull process, you can choose to close your eyes if that assists you in perceiving the energy.

2. Allow the energies of ease, peace and joy with money that you are indulging in and perceiving right now to be in front of you, in your energy bubble. (And remember, if you don't "feel" or sense the energy, you can put that sense of "nothing" into the bubble. It will still work.)

3. Pull energy from all over the universe through the bubble and through you.

4. Increase the relaxation, and keep asking the energy to pull until you feel your heart area warm up or a sensation there.

5. Now, allow trickles of energy to go back out into the world and universe, so all the possibilities matching that energy of ease, peace and joy with money can find you.

6. To finish, reverse the flow so you are pulling energy again. Do one big final pull and let the energy wash through the universe, through the bubble, through your body and out the back of your body, into the universe.

7. And now, you've done the energy pull! Get on with your day, do something enjoyable, take a little break, or if you'd like, read on...

NOTE: I know I've said this before, but I want to reiterate that even if you have trouble doing the exercises as you are reading them, don't be hard on yourself. Just by reading them, you are shifting the energy. Isn't that so cool and easy? If you have yourself convinced you are doing nothing, it's not true. You are not wrong, and you can't do this wrong.

CREATING PEACE WITH MONEY – THE 10% ACCOUNT.

Creating a future where you have peace with money isn't just about eliminating your learned thoughts and feelings around money. It requires pragmatic action, too. Creating a 10% Account is one of the most incredibly dynamic ways to do this.

The 10% account is a simple concept: for every dollar that comes in, you take 10 percent (10 cents) and put that money away for you. You don't spend this money; you don't save it for emergencies or a rainy day. You put it away and watch it grow over time. At some point, you'll reach an amount of money in your 10% account (and that amount is different for each person) where you'll have a true sense of peace with money. When I first heard this tool from Gary Douglas, I would put away my 10% and think, "Why does Gary make us do this? I still don't get it. How rude of him to introduce a way for me to not spend my money when I want to!" Funny that I thought anyone could make me do something I don't truly desire to do!

As my 10% account grew in the following months and years, I noticed my relationship with money changing. The moments of desperate need decreased, money worries became less pervasive, and I became willing to have more money in my life and business.

Several years after starting my 10% account, something interesting occurred. My account reached a certain amount of money where I noticed that the "normal" sense of underlying stress I'd always associated with money was totally gone. I couldn't look at the bank statement and not think myself rich. It was like shifting into a totally new gear, where money now had an abiding sense of peace and relaxation for me.

Now, I am not saying I've become some perfect Zen master with money! I still experience "stuff" around money. However, I now also have an undeniable awareness of myself as the source for possibilities with money. I see the money in my 10% account and acknowledge, "Wow, look at what I created. I have money. I know I can create more money." When you have a sense of possibility in your world with money, you create peace.

ENJOYING MONEY – MONEY FOLLOWS JOY. JOY FOLLOWS MOVEMENT.

How often do you look outside yourself to find answers in life? It's an easy trap to fall into, and it can really mess with your money flows, too! When I ventured into the wide world – going to university and beyond, facilitating Access classes and travelling to amazing places – even though I was having a lot of fun, I also spent a lot of time feeling like a total imposter. I really didn't want to feel that way about myself anymore. I wanted to be someone who was part of a classy and wealthy set of people. I would see other people with beautiful designer items and wearing high-end fashion and conclude that if I also had those expensive items, then I'd come to embody that level of class. It became a "need" in my world to have these fancy things. Having designer bags and fashionable clothes, while nice, didn't magically change my sense of wealth, or my point of view about me. Finally, I had to admit that the sense of wealth and class I desired had to come from me, not from the things I had.

I'd made money the source of power and change in my life, and in the process, made it more valuable and significant than me.

I was making decisions as if I needed money and fine things to create the wealth of my life when all I truly needed was *me.*

I decided to reframe my whole perspective. And here is how I did it:

- First of all, whenever I was making something outside of me more powerful or greater than me, I had to stop and ask myself, *"If I acknowledged me as the source and creative power for everything that shows up in my life, what would I choose?"*
- Second, I recognised that money is not a solution, but it is one of the many *fun by-products* I can generate when I am choosing what truly works for me (not what I decided should work based on what the outside world values).
- Third, money comes far more easily when I choose what is joyful. *Money follows joy.*

Why joy? When you are joyfully engaging with yourself and the world around you, you create a movement of energy that pulls in all kinds of possibilities. Essentially, we function like sharks – we need to keep moving to stay alive, to *enjoy* being alive; and when we make the movement of living a joyful experience, lots of great things, including money, will come to the party.

EXERCISE: A RECIPE FOR LIVING AS THE JOYFUL SOURCE

Do you know what brings you joy? How often do you choose it? Are you willing to discover more and more about what is joyful for you? What if living joyfully was a fundamental element of your day?

Here is how to put it into practice:

Spend an entire day asking, *"What can I choose today that would make me happy right away?"* and choosing *only* what makes you happy.

When this was first suggested to me, I scoffed, "My business productivity will go down the drain if I live my whole day like this." I certainly couldn't imagine it as a sustainable approach for my whole life. But my curiosity won out and one fine day at nine o'clock in the morning, I started asking, "What can I choose today that would make me happy right away?"

My first thought was, "It'd be fun to have a bath," so I did that. Almost the whole time I was in the bath, I felt wrong and bad that I was having a bath at 9 a.m. I also acknowledged that I was having fun. Submerged in my bathtub, I asked the question again, "What else can I do today that would make me happy right away? Oh, I know! I'm going to go to the freezer and get some ice cream." So, I ate ice cream. That was really fun, too, and made me happy. As I was finishing my ice cream, I asked the question again, letting my curiosity lead me.

Eventually I forgot to keep asking the question outright, because I was just in the flow and having a great time. By the evening, I was astonished to realise that I'd accomplished more with my business throughout that day than I had for the past month. My choices created a movement, expansion and enthusiasm that imbued everything I interacted with. I had an amazing day, and I knew that I was only just beginning to discover the possibilities.

I know that sometimes it isn't easy to connect with what would be fun, especially if you are feeling down and it seems like nothing will make a difference. In those times I recommend that you start choosing *something–anything*. Any movement, even getting out of bed and folding your laundry, will start to generate a flow. There are no right or wrong choices. Just choose again and keep going.

Also, take into account the kinds of movement you can enjoy. There is physical movement (moving in ways that your body enjoys – does it like walking, dancing, cartwheeling in the back yard?), energetic movement (like energy pulls and asking questions, or making a choice like choosing gratitude over judgement), and mental movement (such as learning skills, indulging in hobbies and interests, or even watching a TV show).

I get a lot of joy from doing *MasterClass* online video tutorials. I learn cooking from the best chefs, how to do marketing like an expert, how to create amazing flower arrangements, and even master the art of pickling. I also love to educate myself about valuable items like antiques, paintings, and jewelry. I'll research online, but also talk to friends and experts and ask them lots of questions. I also love having a good gossip! I'll call or meet with friends to find out everything that is happening in their lives and talk about where they go, what they do and who they know. To be honest, I will talk to just about anyone and I love making new friends. One of the questions my husband asks me the most is, "Julia, how do you even know this person?!"

Whenever I start to stress about money or slip into making it the answer to some "problem", I know that choosing something fun will help me generate a different possibility. Whether that is picking up the phone, practicing a recipe, or looking around me and being grateful for everything currently in my life.

Joy is created by the movement you choose that makes *you* happy. And remember – money loves to come to the party of joy, not a pity party. If you want more money, choose more joy.

ENERGY PULL #3: REQUESTING THE EXACT AMOUNT OF MONEY YOU DESIRE

Energy pulls really are a space of magic we get to use to create in miraculous ways. And you will make it easier to pull in what you desire by getting very clear on what you require in your financial world.

For this next energy pull, it's time to "do the math" and be aware of *exactly* how much money you are asking for. Is what you are currently asking for enough? Here is how to work it out accurately:

- Add up what it costs to run your life; all your bills, debts, loans, car and business costs and so on, that you are paying each month.
- Add in what you spend or would like to spend on other aspects of your life beyond the basics. This includes clothes, cosmetics, skincare, self-nurturing like massages and facials, trips and holidays, buying gifts for birthdays, eating

out, entertainment, hobbies, self-development courses, all the things that make life fun and enjoyable for you and that you desire to have in your future.

- Add 10% to go into your 10% account.

This is now the new *minimum* amount of money you'll ask for when you do your energy pull. You can review it at any time. Now that you have your amount, let's do the pull:

1. Relax, take a couple of deep breaths, and allow your energy to expand.

2. Get the minimum amount of money you are asking for and put that in the energy bubble in front of you.

3. Add in the sense of ease, peace, and joy of having that amount of money (and more) in your life. Perceive the money swirling around you, piling up in front of you, beside you, behind you. What if it was raining money?

4. Start pulling energy through the whole universe, through you, and through the bubble, from all directions.

5. When your heart area opens up, send out the trickles so the money in all its forms can find you. It's like going out and tapping money everywhere on the shoulder, letting it know you are looking for it.

6. Then to finish, reverse the flow so you are pulling energy again. Do one big final pull and let the energy come through the universe, through the bubble, through your body and out the back of your body, into the universe.

When you do this energy pull, don't get distracted or bogged down in details like worrying if you should be asking for the net or gross income; just ask. And don't just ask for 10 million dollars without being aware of what it costs you to run your life. Look at the amount you can ask for right away that will begin to make a difference in your financial world, it may be easier to create than you think! There is no limit to what you can ask for, so of course ask for all the money, but also get clear on exactly where you are right now, then go forward. Do this energy pull anytime you'd like to create more movement with money.

CHOOSING EASE WITH MONEY - AKA GET COMFORTABLE WITH BEING UNCOMFORTABLE!

Creating a different monetary reality is about committing long term to gaining back parts and pieces of your being one by one and putting yourself in vulnerable situations over and over. I'm not going to sugarcoat this: there'll be some deeply uncomfortable moments. I've had countless times of feeling clueless as I broke out of familiar paths with money. It can be like crawling around in the dark, totally embarrassed, and sure that someone is going to point out and yell, "Look at you, you're a total faker!" I have made some rather interesting choices with money – but with every choice, I've gained incredible awareness that has helped me create something greater. What I'm saying is, you can't really get it wrong. If you are willing, every choice you make will bring great gifts of awareness. So, why not give yourself permission to explore what it would be like to create your world the way you truly enjoy, no matter what?

Let me tell you one of my embarrassing moments that turned out to be a huge contribution. The first expensive ring I ever bought had a large aquamarine stone set in it. When I went home wearing it, my friends laughed at me, saying, "It's far too big!" I looked at the ring and immediately wanted to put it in a drawer because I was suddenly so embarrassed to wear it. That night, I had a conversation with myself: "Okay, do I put this ring in the drawer to gather dust? Or do I build my life to be much bigger, so this ring fits in it?" I wondered what it would be like to wear something like this with ease. What if I could create a life where having a big ring is just the beginning of the elegance and decadence and fun I can have?

If you can get comfortable with being uncomfortable on this adventure, and be kind to you as you go along, you'll have a lot more fun. Relax, and learn to laugh at yourself when you have your insane moments (because we've all learned to be kind of insane when it comes to money, so you are not alone!). Be grateful for you, your choices and what you gain from them. Whether it feels like it in the moment or not, the choices you make will get you closer to the future you desire.

As for my aquamarine ring, I wear it all the time now. I love it! I teach cooking class in it, I do gardening with it on. It is an elegant addition to my life that I enjoy and suits me very well. And it's not because I'm finally fitting some image of being a rich bitch with heaps of jewelry. I'm living a life where I allow myself to be me, to enjoy what I enjoy without the self-judgements of if it is okay to have this, do that, or to live a certain way. The larger life I've created is one where I am included in it, and I'm not concerned or intimidated by what other people think. It isn't about getting it right or wrong, or anything else. It's purely about what works for me, is fun for me, and getting to choose for me, no matter what that looks like, and no matter if it makes sense to anyone else.

QUICK RECAP

Phew! That was quite a chapter. We covered a lot of ground and discussed so many tools, even I'm impressed. Let's do a quick re-cap:

Changing your energy around money is not an overnight exercise, and you are going to have to be brave, because it might just make you an anomaly to those around you. However, if you are willing to pull more money into your life and have the adventure of discovering what you can add that will invite more wealth, there is nothing that can stop you.

Pay attention to the energies that come up for you when you think about money. Ask, "Who do these belong to?" Most, if not all, of the points of view and feelings and energies you have around money were taught to you. If you got to choose, what energies would you have around money? Get the sense of the energetic relationship you'd like to have with money, and do energy pulls to invite that to be your life.

Money is a by-product of the movement you choose that brings you joy. Make it your daily practice to ask, "What would be fun for me? What can I choose that would make me happy today?" and then choose those things.

Know exactly how much money you'd like to make each month, minimum, and do energy pulls for that amount of money, as often as you like! And remember, don't make money the source or the answer to your life. *You* are the creative source of your life. It is your choice that creates.

Challenges and uncomfortable things will come up. There may be "aha!" moments and "oh darn" moments and some really confronting times. This is great, because you are finally becoming aware of the limiting points of views you've held yourself back with, and you can now look at what different choice you might like to make. Just like when I bought my big beautiful ring, ask yourself, "Am I limiting what I am willing to have to fit inside a smaller life? Or am I creating a greater life that includes everything I'd really like to have?"

CHAPTER 11
Business

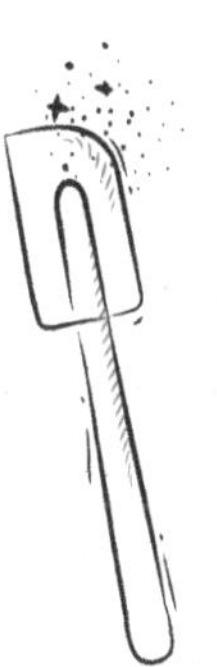

Starting my first facilitation business using the energy pulls created an adventure that showed me that magic is truly possible when you are willing to ask, act and receive. By the time I'd graduated university, I had already created a lot. And, like I mentioned back in Chapter Four, the time came when I was ready to move on. I remember it so clearly. I'd not long graduated from university, and I was once again scraping ice off my car windscreen on a bone-numbingly cold day when I thought, "I'm done. I'm ready for something different. Also, I need to move somewhere warmer!" I immediately began to wonder, *what else is truly possible for me?*

What else is possible?® is another simple Access tool that I believe deserves a premium place in everyone's "creating magic" toolkit. Wondering what else is possible with no other thought or caveat is a beautiful energy – and it is a possibility-creator on steroids because it opens you up to *anything* and *everything* changing, if you are willing.

Not long after, I spoke to a friend from Vancouver who was living in a beautiful apartment complex in Coal Harbour, one of the most expensive neighbourhoods in Canada. The apartments in her building overlooked incredible views of snow-peaked mountains and the ocean. They also rented from $3000 per month, which for a single girl at the time, was an obscene amount. But there was *something* in the energy of choosing to move there that I could not deny myself, so I pulled a "Baba Florence" and decided that I was going to make it happen. I also decided to apply for a larger apartment on the 21st floor, with two bedrooms instead of just one because it more matched the energy I was looking to have in my life.

When it came time to put in my rental application, I didn't have all the financial evidence to show that I could afford the rental payments, so I made a call to Gary. I'd put him down as a contact on my application and asked him if he'd contribute some of his magic to having this all work out for me with ease. The real estate office never called him, but I got approval, and I moved to my beautiful apartment with the stunning views.

One of my first thoughts was, okay great, I'm sorted for the first month, but how the heck was I going to keep up the rent payment every month? I'd just moved across the country, away from the business base I'd created. I also knew I had a lot of creative juice and a commitment to truly live and take in everything life had to offer, so I went out daily to discover the streets and treasures of Vancouver.

I interacted with all kinds of people through my business but also just in my day to day exploring. I became more present with my business, too. Every day I would ask, "*What else can I add to my business?*" and played with a ton of new ideas. I wanted to keep connected with the people I'd met and worked with no matter where I was in the world, so I started creating more online classes via Zoom. To my surprise, it really took off, and I started to make a lot more money than I'd ever anticipated. It was an explosion of possibilities that didn't just end there.

Moving to Vancouver was a choice that facilitated me to expand my business and have so many of the adventures I'd been dreaming of since I was little, and there were other magical and unexpected benefits I hadn't predicted. During this time, I started dating Anthony, and he'd sometimes come to visit with the kids. Having chosen the larger apartment, I not only had the space to host them comfortably, but I could see that living in this beautiful area gave the kids a sense that I was someone who was put together and committed to creating their future. I think it inspired them and garnered enthusiasm and respect for having me as a mom. I got to see how my choices not only contributed to me, but the people in my life, which was just so cool! Truly, how does it get any better?

A DIFFERENT RECIPE FOR BUSINESS

By giving me the energy pulls, Gary was inviting me to BE the energy that will invite everything I desire to show up *in my entire life, including my business.*

Since then, I've come to acknowledge how much creating a limitless business is about being willing to have *your* reality and let others into it as well. In fact, you have to be willing for others to bask in the glow of your reality if a business born from your creativity is to thrive. When you do, you are essentially being you out in the world without apology, which invites others to choose that for themselves, as well.

Personally, I would love to see a world where business is all about getting to be you, enjoying your unique capacities, and where you get to change the world and make money. Since that is quite different from the usual "how to create a business" education, I'm going to share with you some tools for creating business that expands your life:

- Asking questions
- Chaos (don't worry, I'll explain!)
- Engagement
- Gratitude (Yes, that again.)
- Invigoration

STUCK IN BUSINESS? ASK A QUESTION.

What difference and gift are you in your business, that you do not acknowledge?

I was in a total business rut the day my amazing husband said to me, "Julia, get back to the energy of you in business. The way I see you in business when you are being a success is the energy of a fairy walking barefoot in the garden. That's the way you are. Stop trying to make yourself normal and stop trying to make yourself wrong. Just go out and play and have fun. That's going to increase things for you."

And he was absolutely correct. Somewhere along the way, I'd stopped asking questions and I'd stopped having fun. I'd received one or two critical emails from people, and allowed that to shut me down. I'd gone into the wrongness of me and my business and was trying to fix it, rather than create it.

Anthony's wonderful acknowledgement of my energy with business was not a definition of, "You must float and giggle and skip around and be 'fairy-like' and if you are not doing that, you are not being you in business." Being the gift of you in your business isn't about finding a new fixed idea of what, when, where, how, why, and who to be. It is about the energy you are when you let go of all the definitions and start enjoying the unlimited things you are capable of creating.

When things aren't exactly as we want, or we have a goal we'd really like to achieve in business, our tendency is to control more to try and force a result. You'll know when you are doing this in your life or business when you get unhappy or stressed, or you keep looking for the right thing to do to avoid pitfalls or solve problems or get obsessed with not making mistakes. Instead, what would work a lot better is to do the opposite - control *less*, and start asking more questions.

When Anthony reminded me to start acknowledging and appreciating my difference in business and choose more from the space of magic, I knew I needed to start asking questions that gave me new and greater possibilities. Not answers and not solutions. I started asking:

"What am I capable of that I don't even know I'm capable of?"

"What's possible here I have not considered?"

"What would be *fun* for me to choose?"

I cannot tell you the amount of times the most phenomenal change in my life and business has come from asking a question as simple as, "What else is possible?" Especially when I'm approaching it as if I had total amnesia with my business. By doing this, I'm hitting the full "reset" button, so nothing from that past impinges on my creative energy today and in the future. When you let go of everything the business was yesterday, the possibilities are free to flow today, and true *chaos* can ensue.

And why on earth would you want *chaos* in your business? I'm so glad you asked. Please, allow me to explain!

CHAOS... AND A SMIDGEN OF ORDER

There have been plenty of times I've judged myself as naïve regarding the "business world", and yet I've also noticed the advantage of approaching everything from a totally open space of question and curiosity. The times I play and follow the energy rather than the logic, is when the really cool stuff shows up. Another word for choosing from this open energy is, you may have guessed it – *chaos*.

Chaos often gets a bad reputation, mostly because it is one of those words whose definition has become confused with other energies, like *havoc*. In modern times, havoc and chaos are used kind of interchangeably, to describe destruction and disruption. However, they're actually very different.

Havoc has its root in the Old French word, *havot*, meaning "plundering or pillaging." *Chaos*, on the other hand, is an even older word, with its roots in Greek. Its original form, *khaos,* means vast chasm, or void. In other words, total space. *Khaos* was used by the Greeks to describe the unidentifiable primordial elements of creation and, in their mythology, was the name of the first creator being. *Chaos theory* is a modern scientific term used to describe the study of "patterns" in the universe whose outcomes cannot be predicted, no matter how much data you collect, because even the smallest change creates infinite variables and possibilities. Chaos is the energy by which the universe – and we as beings – function. It is unbound creative energy that has no structure. When you allow yourself to function from chaos, you are truly letting the magic in and of you to show up, often as wonderful things and occurrences that you cannot track or explain.

Having said all this, there is a time and place for a bit of structure or *order*. Order is kind of the opposite energy to chaos, and it has its uses. However, a little goes a long way.

I am an extremely organised person. I like to have some order in my business. I like to make sure things are moving along, that all the little elements are taken care of. I love having systems in place for things to run smoothly. However, when I create too much order and start to limit and control things (such as micro-managing or getting fixated on getting things done at a certain time or looking a particular way), I start killing the business. Rather than a smidgen of order to keep things rolling smoothly, too much order will strangle things into stagnation.

Most of us will do about 99% more order in business than is necessary. Let's change that up now and do an energy pull to invite more chaos.

ENERGY PULL #4: INVITING CHAOS

This one's a quickie, but feel free to indulge and immerse yourself in this energy for as long as you desire!

1. Assume your preferred energy pull position, and relax your body.
2. Breathe and allow your energy to expand until the space in your body and beyond feels light and expansive.
3. Ask: *What energy of chaos can I be and invite into my business?*
4. Put the energy of that question out in front of you into the energy bubble.
5. Pull energy from every direction, through the energy bubble and through you.
6. As your heart warms up, reverse the flow and send trickles back out to the universe.
7. Do a final pull through the entire universe, through you, and invite the energy of chaos to imbue your molecules. Enjoy!

TRUE ENGAGEMENT

Let's get engaged!

I'm not talking about marriage, in case you were wondering. In this context, I'm talking about the kind of engagement that is about you being yourself openly in the world and not hiding from anyone or anything. It is about contributing to others and allowing them to contribute to you.

On a pragmatic level, engagement is being present and curious in your interactions.

For the sake of expanding your business with a lot more ease, here are two lists to get you clear on what engagement is and is not:

Engagement is:

- Talking to people in person
- Talking to people on the phone
- Asking questions, listening, and being interested in those people and what they are doing.
- Asking yourself, "Where can I go and who can I talk to today to keep me on my way?" and taking action.

Engagement is NOT:

- Emails
- Text messages, live streams, or voice messaging. If you aren't talking with them in real time, it isn't engagement. Messages are not communication; they are information exchange. No exceptions.
- Talking about yourself only, and not asking people questions about themselves.

ARE YOU WILLING TO HAVE 100 CONVERSATIONS?

I've heard Gary say hundreds of times to people, "If you want to increase your sales, customers, clients or business, pick up the phone and call people. When you call them, don't tell them anything about you, ask them about what they are doing. If they don't ask you a question, don't tell them anything. If they do ask you, you can say, "Oh I'm doing ______, do you know anyone who might be interested?"

Not so long ago, I chose to make 100 phone calls over a period of a few weeks. I don't mean I dialled 100 numbers. I had 100 *conversations* with people over the phone. I called them and asked them about their lives and experiences. I'm naturally curious (you might recall that I love a good gossip!) so I had a fascinating time finding out about people all over the world. And... something else occurred that I had not expected.

The level of gratitude that flowed back to me for calling and caring about these people and their lives with no strings attached was phenomenal. In the weeks and months after, there was this energy of being connected to these people and contributed to that continued to flow into my life. People would call or message, asking if I was coming to a class they were attending, or reach out, thanking me for the energy I am in their lives. Maybe people had done this before and I hadn't truly acknowledged it, but something fundamental changed for me with this. The gratitude I was able to both gift and receive went through the roof. After that, I was invited to do a class in Indonesia by a woman I'd not yet met in person. I was treated with such regard. It was a wonderful experience that gifted so much to me personally.

Realising that people were so willing to gift to me also invited me to acknowledge, without a doubt, that I am a contribution. That was super exciting, but also a bit uncomfortable, because I had to stretch beyond my self-judgements and not find some reason to reject or downplay the kindness and gratitude being flowed to me.

On that note, I'd like to invite you to stretch your no-judgement muscles and develop your superpower of gifting and receiving gratitude.

HAVING AND RECEIVING GRATITUDE

In my early days of dating Anthony, I was making about $6,000 USD a month. I didn't think it was anything to boast about, but Anthony thought it was cool and told my father-in-law proudly, "Julia makes $6000 a month." For a moment I was kind of embarrassed, but then I questioned my point of view. Instead of making myself wrong, and thinking I should be doing more, I said to myself, "Actually it *is* cool and amazing that I generate that. I'm grateful to make that amount of money. Why wouldn't I be?"

In a class I run called *Healing Your Bank Account*, I invite my participants to play with choosing gratitude for every dollar their business makes:

Look at the money you have right now. That might be the cash in your wallet, or the amount of dollars on your bank statement.

Even if you have $10 in your wallet or bank account right now, look at that money. If it's cash, you can even hold it in the palm of your hand. Look at that money and acknowledge, "I created this. This is in my life right now because of me. This is a super cool $10 bill. How lucky am I to have this?"

As a result of doing this little exercise every day, the class participants witnessed their lives growing dynamically. Why? Because gratitude will change the energy in your life in a very big way.

Gratitude may seem like this puny, insignificant tool, but in truth it will rewire the way that everything in your life functions. *Gratitude is a powerful foundation from which you can build, create and expand anything in your life.*

Choose gratitude for the cash in your hand, your wallet, the amount of money in your bank, even the bills and running costs for your business. Practice being grateful for your entire business, and for you as the creator of your business. Wow, you created all of that. Now, what more can you create that you never even considered?

At this point in my own adventure, it has become undeniable to me that gratitude changes things. When I'm grateful for whatever I'm creating, regardless of the amount of money, both my business and income have a way of expanding beyond my expectations. Business gets a lot harder when I stop being grateful and start thinking that everything that I'm doing is a terrible idea, that I'm somehow wrong for what I'm doing, or that no amount of money I make is ever enough.

As you choose to have more gratitude for yourself, you'll become more capable of receiving the gratitude of others, too. Gifting and receiving gratitude exponentialises what can be contributed to your life, business and future. So, if you'd like to be more successful in business, or with anything, start with being more grateful for you.

BORED? FRUSTRATED? TIME TO INVIGORATE!

Have you ever had those moments when you just know you are creating drama in your life because you haven't given yourself something better to do?

I distinctly remember a conversation I had with Gary where I was so upset, having what I thought was a very serious and major problem with someone in my life, and his response was, "Why does this even matter to you?" Umm, excuse me? What is *that* supposed to mean?

Gary said, "Right now you are so bored, you are creating problems. You've got to do whatever it takes to get invigorated in your life. It doesn't matter what you do, but you need to go do something. If you have to streak naked down your street, then do it."

I laughed as I recognised the degree of thrill he was getting me to acknowledge, and how much that was not currently in my life. My thoughts trailed off, and suddenly I remembered a time when I was a young teenager on the farm. During sleepovers, my sister, my friends and I would get completely naked, wrap ourselves in towels and go outside under the moon. We would throw the towels on the ground and run naked up and down my long country lane. With the mammoth spruce trees towering above us on a crisp Canadian summer night, the air felt so nice on my naked body. And yes - I was the one who came up with that idea. That was living. That was invigorating. Now, I was trying so hard to get my life right, be a good wife, mom and business owner, that I wasn't doing many things like that. When I asked myself, "What would create an immense invigoration of my life and living?" the idea that occurred to me seemed so weird (and I bet you are thinking, "What could be weirder than running around naked?), I almost didn't want to admit it.

"Gary, I think I want to be a waitress again. I loved it so much previously, and when I started doing my Access business, I was actually a bit sad that I wasn't going to waitress anymore. Sometimes I even feel like I need to get that out of my system before I can truly move forward."

"Cool. Go do it."

That same day, I rang my sister to help me put my resumé together. Then, I put on a nice dress, drove thirty minutes to my favourite restaurant and asked for a job. They took one look at me, didn't so much as glance at the resume, and hired me on the spot. I ended up working there for seven months. I had a blast! I was engaging with people all day, running around serving multiple tables. I was so present and alive with every customer I served, asking them questions about their lives, and seeing each person for who they were in ways I don't know if anyone in their life had before. Endless amounts of people told me I was the best waitress they had ever had. When we had customers from international countries, chances are I had already facilitated in that country at one time or another. When you facilitate in a foreign country it moves you to understand a culture in a way almost nothing else can. I made them feel so welcome because I knew intimate details about their homeland.

The restaurant owner was a brilliant guy from Australia, and it was fun to watch how he ran his business. I got paid something, too, which was great, but that wasn't really the point. The energies that choosing that job contributed to me exploded into every area of my life. Every area of my life seemed to flow easier and become more... explosive (in a good way).

I also learned that even if you are an entrepreneur, with big dreams, businesses, and all kinds of things you want to create, it's also okay to go get a job. It moves energy and creates possibilities. *When you don't judge it, you can choose anything that will contribute to the expansion of your future.*

What can you choose right now that would invigorate you? Are there choices you have avoided because you've already judged them out of your universe? I'd concluded years ago that since I was doing my own business, I would have to permanently "move on" from waitressing. Interesting judgement I had there. I'm so glad I got over it.

Two more things before we move on from here:

1. Please don't underestimate the contribution of choosing what makes you invigorated and enthusiastic in life. In truth, when you are invigorated and enjoying your life, you are being the energy pull that brings the possibilities to your door. Isn't that amazing?

2. Allow yourself to keep moving and changing when you know it is time. After seven months of waitressing, I was different. I was generating invigoration in all kinds of ways I hadn't before chosen, and I knew my job had done its job!

ENERGY PULL #5: UNIVERSE, SHOW ME...

It's truly amazing how many possibilities exist in the realm of business, and I hope you are curious and enthused to play with these energies to see what magic you can create. Remember, the universe has your back in all of this. Let's do an energy pull and invite the contribution of the universe to play with you and your business:

1. Relax your body.
2. Breathe.
3. Expand your energy until you create a beautiful sense of space in your body and you feel it relax even more.
4. When you are ready, tap into the energies that we've covered in this chapter, and ask the universe to contribute to more of it showing up for you, with ease.
5. If you want, you can ask it like this:
    - *Universe, show me the gift of me in business that I've never acknowledged*
    - *Universe, show me what question and chaos I can be*
    - *Universe, show me what true engagement is*

- *Universe, show me what being and receiving gratitude with my business is like*
- *Universe, show me how much fun and invigoration I can choose and be*

6. Put the energy in front of you, into the energy bubble, and pull energy in from every direction, through you and the bubble.
7. When your heart warms up, reverse the flow and send trickles back out to the universe, along with your curiosity for what more you can be, receive and enjoy.
8. Reverse the flow again into a final pull, and as you do, ask how much more contribution can you receive from the universe today that will keep you (and your business) on your way?

EXTRA QUICK RECAP

Creating your life and business is a continuously expanding adventure of creation, and being you is the essential, foundational ingredient. The moment you try forsaking yourself to do business "right", you'll know it, because things will suddenly become a lot harder and less fun. To create a business that truly works for you, these are you new go-to tools:

- Question
- Chaos
- Engagement
- Gratitude
- Invigoration

Think of this chapter as your friend who reminds you of the gift you are, and invites you into the dynamic curiosity, playfulness and energy of *you* that will get your life and business flowing, no matter what.

CHAPTER 12
Body

Let's return momentarily to the time I was living in my beautiful apartment complex in Vancouver, on the 21st floor. Not only could I look out of my windows to see the mountains and ocean, I was also situated by a National Historic Site called Stanley Park, a 400-hectare (1000-acre) old growth forest, boasting half a million trees, many of which are over 400 years old. Species like Douglas Fir, Red Cedar and Big Leaf Maple tower up to heights of 76 meters (250 feet), with enormous trunks the length of a full-grown crocodile. It is a truly stunning place, and yet there were stretches of time I didn't go out and would spend days inside the apartment. Some afternoons, for no apparent reason, I would feel depressed.

One particularly miserable evening, I got so fed up I said, "Okay Julia, you have two choices: descend further into the depths of despair or get up and *do something*." I looked outside and decided to take a nighttime bicycle ride around the park.

It was... incredible.

The bike path took me on a breathtaking two-hour route through the trees, then out around the edge of the park, where it was met by ocean. At one point, the path on my left dropped directly to the water, while on my right, snowcapped mountains rose beyond the treetops.

I rode along in awe of my surroundings, amazed at how quickly my despair had shifted to elation. I felt a profound connection to everything, and joy coursed through every cell of my body. How did I miss such enchantment that was literally at my doorstep this whole time? I began to wonder if the depression I'd been feeling was really just my body's way of telling me, "Julia, you are surrounded by beauty and magic, can we please go out and enjoy it, move through it, and BE part of it?"

I started going on regular nightly rides, experiencing new wonderment each time. I would cycle under the superstructure of the Lions Gate Bridge, a huge 1500-meter suspension bridge that spanned the water, connecting the main city of Vancouver with its northern municipalities. Whenever I passed under the bridge's super-structure, I would look up and marvel at its viridian green magnificence. I'd feel the wind, hear the ocean, and be embraced by the sound of crickets singing in the trees.

I created some of the most magical nights of my life out on that path. I thanked my body for persisting with me and inviting me to the possibilities it was aware of that I had been ignoring. I am grateful to me for listening to my body, too. Through this experience, I gained incredible awareness of the ways my body does its best to show me the *gloriousness* that is possible with embodiment. By "embodiment" I mean the beautiful combination of you, the being, in partnership with your body to create an experience of living on this planet that is truly magnificent.

You might have guessed by now that this chapter isn't going to just be about your physical body being healthy and feeling good. It includes that of course, but it is also much, much more.

ASK YOUR BODY ABOUT YOUR BODY

I'd love to dive into a unique and future-altering conversation with our bodies right here and now, because it is beyond amazing what your body can contribute to you and show you if you start including its unique awareness in your life.

Have you ever sat down with your body and said, *"Hey body, I know I've judged you and tried to control you and tell you what is best for you, but now I'm going to stop that and start asking you about you. Body, what is it that you desire, what is it that you are trying to show me, and what do you know that I don't?"?*

If you haven't, would you be willing to start right away?

If my experience in Vancouver taught me anything at all, it is that my body is aware of what will help me thrive in my *whole life*, not just physically. Nurturing your body nurtures your life. If you don't include your body in the conversation of everything concerning your body, you'll exclude a huge amount of awareness from your body of what would work for it, and for you.

Think about this for a minute: If you were just a being floating around without a body, there are things you would not require. You wouldn't need a house, a bed, a car, money, clothes or food. With a body, however, these things suddenly become relevant. If these things are for your body, and your body has its own awareness, what would happen if you asked your body what it wanted regarding each of those things?

EXERCISE: WHERE DO YOUR POINTS OF VIEW ABOUT BODIES COME FROM?

You've been taught by outside sources your whole life about what your body needs. Let's start unpacking that a little further.

What points of view about health, eating, movement, strength, disease, pain, aging, and sex have you accumulated throughout your life?

Take a few minutes to write down your thoughts and beliefs about your body, and bodies in general either here or in your own notebook. You may need more paper once you get started. Take your time and really go for it. I'll wait.

____

____

____

____

____

____

____

Once you have noted down a few points of view (or a lot), read them over again and ask yourself: *Have any of these points of view I've formed come from my own body's awareness? Or have they come from someone or somewhere else?*

You might notice that most, if not all these points of view, don't come from your body. That's pretty normal in a world where we've never been told that our bodies have their own knowing. And if some of the perspectives you listed above were moments when you listened to your body as it showed you something different – that is truly awesome – and how does it get even better than that?

This exercise is not intended to make you judge yourself. Every time you gain more awareness for yourself, that's something to celebrate! Because now, new possibilities can begin.

Start by giving your body some space to show you what it knows is possible that you've never considered. Think of something that is going on with your body right now. Instead of trying to find the solution to fix that problem, ask:

"Body, what do you know that I don't that would change all of this?"

"Body, can you help me take care of myself?"

Ask this question and get into the habit of having frequent conversations with your body where your body's awareness is included. You won't be able to predict what shows up, because it's not about seeking answers and results. Just know that these questions are opening a door to a whole new universe of possibilities, and be open to receiving them.

ENERGY PULL #6: BODY, SHOW ME HOW TO TAKE CARE OF MYSELF

What fun can you and your body have exploring the possibilities of a joyful embodiment together? Let's use the energy pull to invite your body's awareness and all the magical things it has been desiring to gift you for a long time. I am really excited about this particular energy pull; I can't wait to see what can unfold when you let your body care for you and contribute to your life.

1. Find a comfy spot. As you sit or lie down, tune into your body and its sensations. Is there tension you can now invite to release and relax?

2. Expand out far beyond the edges of your body and allow your body to melt as the space between your molecules expands.

3. Ask these questions, and put the energy of your request into the energy bubble in front you:

   - *Body, please show me how to take care of myself.*

   - *Body, please show me what you know that would make embodiment far more wonderful than I can possibly anticipate?*

4. Pull massive amounts of energy through the whole universe, through the bubble, through your body and out the back of your body.

5. Keep flowing the energy through your body, through every single pore of your body like a big river of light. Pull through the universe, through the energy bubble, and through you.

6. And now let little trickles out to any beings, any energy, any person, anything that can contribute and invite it to show up in your life with ease.
7. After you have done this, reverse the flow and start pulling energy again until you feel your heart open and you and your body receiving.

CREATING PEACE WITH YOUR BODY

This is the part of the story where I admit I'm not perfect. Wait, I feel like I've done that already. Okay, so this is the part of the story where I tell you about the adventure of creating something different with my body that I was only willing to explore when my body was basically hitting me over the head with a frying pan.

Some years ago, I developed quite strong food allergies. I wasn't always sure what foods would set off an allergy attack, so I just got used to handling it and sometimes feeling terrible for a few hours after eating.

A turning point came when I found some old diaries I'd written at the age of nineteen, when I first started using Access tools to ask for change with my body. I'd written things like, "I'd like to not get sick all the time." I had developed coping mechanisms without realising it. At that time I would avoid anything and anyone that might expose me to situations where I'd catch seasonal colds and flus. I'd mentally prepare for my body to get run down and sick after bouts of travelling or intense work. I'd eat more candy than my body wanted, and would find any justification for feeling sick after, instead of listening to what my body was telling me. I'd used a lot of tools to help me have greater ease with all of this, but I hadn't really acknowledged how much my life, my energy, and my sense of well-being was being affected. And I was definitely ignoring how much my body was trying to show me something different. It wanted to thrive and have a much greater sense of peace and relaxation, while I'd decided that feeling just a little bit better was enough.

It isn't just me who has done this. So many of us have things going on with our body and lives that we decide is tolerable as long as we slightly improve or develop good coping mechanisms. We don't ask for something *much* greater. But our bodies do. They are saying, *"Hello. There is a universe of peace, joy and relaxation that we can create together, will you please allow me to show you?"*

With the allergies getting worse and finally acknowledging how long I'd actually been having difficulty with my body, I began to look at what I'd been avoiding for a long time: changing my relationship with food.

One of the things I knew my body wasn't handling well was dairy. This was quite a conundrum for me, since ice cream is pretty much my favourite food on the whole planet. Well, it was *my* favourite food, but it didn't seem to be my body's, so I began to wonder what points of view I had about it?

The next morning in the shower (where I do lots of profound wondering) I asked myself, *"What are all the points of view I have about not being able to eat ice cream?"* Observing the tsunami of intense thoughts, feelings and emotions that surged through my world at that one question was both astounding and enlightening!

I realised that I had formed hundreds and hundreds of points of view about ice cream – none of which were about eating it when my body desired to eat it. Over the next few days, I repeated this shower-question process with all my favourite foods, like pizza, lasagne, chocolate and many of the foods I grew up with.

Considering that it is our bodies that taste, chew, ingest, digest and deal with all the molecular components of the food, it is quite amazing that we, the beings, form opinions about foods we love. The question we never ask is, "Hey body, would *you* like to eat this? And if so, when and how much would you like to eat?"

When I began to acknowledge all the points of view I had accumulated about foods, especially the ones that I decided I loved, I realised that I had never really asked my body what kind of food it truly liked to eat. I had gone through the motions of asking, but how could I really listen when I'd already made so many decisions about these foods for other reasons outside of my body? It was like white noise that constantly got in the way of acknowledging what my body was whispering to me. Acknowledging the judgements I'd created around food and letting them go made it a whole lot easier to let my body do the choosing.

I knew that if I really wanted to create sustainable changes with my body, I was going to have to give up the control and all the points of view that I'd been holding onto and ask:

Body, what kind of food do you actually desire to eat?

Body, can you show me what kind of food you'd like to eat, and show me when you want me to change and eat something different?

We learn to develop a *lot* of judgements about food, dieting, gut health and so on. The only way you will truly navigate through this polarised minefield with ease is to ask your body to show you what it desires. The point here is: ask your body about your body.

I discovered my body was asking for different foods from what I'd been giving it most of the time. I learned to cook new recipes, make my own fermented foods, and to choose food from the point of view of asking my body what would make it sing with happiness. I noticed food cravings disappear and a peace and calm with food started to permeate my world in ways I didn't even know could be possible.

EXERCISE: ASKING WHAT YOUR BODY KNOWS

Bodies have their own knowing and their own timeline for change as well. When I started changing my food choices, I knew I had to be patient and let my body lead the way. That meant letting go of the control and the projections and expectations I had about what it would take, what I'd have to do, and for how long. I was going to have to let my body show me, and get my mind out of the way. I also wrote down all the things I'd like to change with my body and asked my body to contribute to that change.

Please write down the top 3–5 things you'd like to change with your body right now:

____

____

____

____

____

____

____

Ask your body, *"Body, what do you know that would help me change these with ease?"*

And now comes the tricky part – relax, and let your body show you a greater possibility.

There is an Access class I facilitate called the 3-Day Body Class. In this class, there is a manual with more than 60 hands-on energetic body processes. One of the rules of this class is that when you partner up to exchange body processes, you ask your partner's body, not the person themselves, to choose the process. Basically, you allow yourself to lightly "tune in" to their body and then run the body process that leaps out at you from the book. No thinking. Just choose. The amount of resistance that people can have to trusting their bodies in this process can be quite interesting!

Seeing this occur in my classes really demonstrated to me the degree to which we'll control and resist our body's awareness, even as we aim to create a greater connection with our bodies. Of course, I have demonstrated my own ability to resist dynamically with my story above, so I just want to say once more, please don't judge you. You're changing some very ingrained ways of functioning.

Each step you take to listen to your body, to ask your body, even to acknowledge how much you avoid listening to your body is a success, because you are choosing what you've not chosen before.

Your body truly desires more for you. It desires a greater future for you than you do. It will create itself based on your judgements and limitations if that is what you insist upon it, because it doesn't believe you are wrong or bad for any of that. But it will also keep trying to show you other possibilities.

We have kind and patient bodies. We have magical bodies. Together, you and your body can be a formidable team, so go ahead and ask for everything you desire with your body. At the same time, ask your body to show you what it knows that you don't. Your body would like to show you a totally different way of being that includes a level of peace, joy and gratitude in your life that you never imagined possible. Are you willing to have it all, and more?

ENERGY PULL #7: CREATING GREATER TOGETHER

Asking for the awareness and contribution of your body is a whole new universe. Learning to receive what your body is trying to show you will take time and practice, and in all honesty, you'll have times when judgements and beliefs will rear their ugly heads to make you doubt your own sanity, but please, trust you, and trust your body. Be willing to look at each and every point of view that comes up and say, "Oh that's an interesting point of view I learned, but I wonder what my body's point of view is? Does it even have a point of view about this?".

And of course, add a potent energy pull to invite your body to contribute what it knows is possible:

1. Relax and expand your energy out across the universe.
2. Allow the barriers or tension in your world and your body to begin to dissipate.
3. Can you expand even more?
4. Invite the energy of gratitude to flow through you. Flow it towards you, through you and out the back of you. Keep flowing gratitude through your body with beautiful flowing rivers of wonder and appreciation. You can even say, *"Thanks body, for sticking with me! Thanks for being here with me today."*
5. Pull all of that gratitude through your body and out the back of you into the universe.

6. From this space, allow your barriers to drop even more as you play with this question:
    - *Body, what future would you like to create that I have never considered?*
7. Put that energy and request out in front of you, into the energy bubble.
8. Pull energy from all over the universe, through the bubble, through you, through your magical body. Keep pulling from all directions until you sense that warmth in your heart area.
9. Reverse the flow a little and trickle energy out to all the things that will contribute to you and your body having total communion – that space of peace, ease, no judgement and total nurturing.
10. Reverse the flow once again, and pull energy through the universe, through the energy bubble, through your body, and back out into the universe.

THE GLORY OF EMBODIMENT

Growing up, harvest time was the best time of the year. There were extra seasonal field workers to feed, so I would spend hours alongside my mom in the kitchen, helping prepare lunches and suppers to take out to the field. My mom would cook hot dishes like beef stroganoff, lasagna or roast beef and gravy. She'd often make Ukrainian and Polish delights like nalysnyky (Ukrainian crepes filled with cottage cheese, covered in cranberry sauce from cranberries we had picked off of the cranberry bushes ourselves) and pierogi (Polish style dumplings). She'd prepare a huge pile of mashed potatoes, and there was always a wonderful dessert. Then, we'd fill the car to the brim with lawn chairs and cardboard boxes packed with our whimsical variety of dishes and drinks (Coke for Dad, Pepsi for Uncle Wayne, and Ginger Ale for the "healthy" option, as well as big jars of hot black tea with honey) along with china plates, metal flatware, and cloth napkins. No plastic or paper picnicware here! We'd drive the truck out to the workers, where both family and workers would gather for the feast.

As we bound across the field, being jostled along with all the picnic items in the back, I'd listen to the porcelain dishes clanking inside their cardboard boxes and revel in the feeling of being with the earth, the sky, and everything in between, anticipating all the fun we'd have seeing our older cousin Larissa, whom my sister and I idolised because she was so worldly and cool, talking with the cute younger farm hands, and laughing at the stories the older gentlemen would regale us with.

The joy of these seasonal suppers on the field have made such an impression, that to this day, I am obsessed with creating epic picnics. I have a special picnic checklist, so I never forget anything. That list includes proper crystal stemware, my favourite Ralph Lauren knives and forks, fine china, and beautiful linen tea cloths and napkins, all packed in a proper wicker picnic basket. The picnic feast always has a specialty cocktail, like a peach basil martini, and I put on an amazing spread with meats, salads, breads, you name it. The joy of abundant, elegant and sumptuous picnics with the hedonistic experience of drinking from crystal and eating off porcelain plates whilst stretched out on a beautiful rug, shaded by the branches of a glorious tree, is something that contributes so much magic to my life.

I feel so lucky to have had such a wonder-filled childhood from my point of view. It was my first awareness of the incredible capacity I had to nourish people around me with food and atmosphere.

When I realised my body was asking for different food than what I'd been feeding it, it was confronting at first. In some ways it felt like a betrayal to all the things I'd grown up with. But the celebration and the glory of the feasts and the picnics were not ever about the exact food ingredients – that could easily change. It was the bringing together of the elements of beauty and happiness that created the adventure of living for me – the movement and bustling energy, being out on the beautiful earth, spending time with beautiful people, and of course the food we'd prepared being enjoyed. Changing my relationship with my body around food really showed me that I could still have the beautiful associations with my Ukrainian Canadian heritage, the wonderful memories of being with my Mom in the kitchen and out on the field with my family and friends.

Cooking and having picnics and parties are still some of my favourite ways to enjoy the gift of embodiment.

Since listening to my body more about the food it enjoys, I've expanded my culinary skills, discovered flavours that make my body hum with pleasure, and I've generated a greater sense of peace and exuberance that extends into all areas of my life. I've also become more willing to receive awareness from my body, because I can trust it is always showing me the way to something far greater than I'm even looking at most of the time.

QUICK RECAP WITH ONE ADDITION

The abundance of possibilities for peace, expansion and aliveness with your body is beyond mind boggling. It is totally different from the learned reality of judging, criticising and controlling our bodies. To truly enjoy having a body, you are going to have to be willing to be magnificently different from pretty much everyone you know, and actually begin to ask your body questions about itself and about what it desires to gift you. I don't know about you, but I think having your body as your BFF (Best Friend Forever) is actually pretty cool. If you choose this, maybe it'll catch on with the people around you and they'll start choosing it, too. Who knows?

Including your body with questions, curiosity, joy and gratitude opens an infinite universe of magic with embodiment. I hope you and your body will have a lot of fun creating with this chapter over and over.

While I have done my best to give you a lot to play with, I still feel that what I've covered here is barely the beginning. On that note, I would love to recommend one of the most healing books I've read about bodies, called *Body Whispering*, by my dear friend Dr. Dain Heer. It is a beautiful exploration with all kinds of miraculousness for you and body.

CHAPTER 13

Relationship

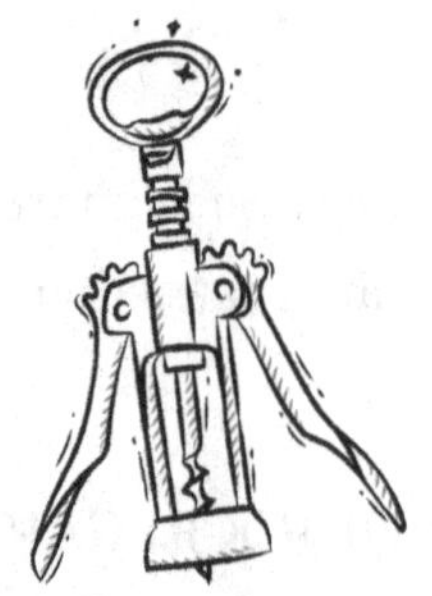

I'm going to open this chapter with a confession: for as long as I can remember, I have loooooved love! I had my first celebrity crush at three years old, when I saw Jerry Seinfeld on TV. His lanky Jewishness set my toddler heart a-flutter. In kindergarten, I became smitten with a very handsome 6th grader named Patrick who used to greet me kindly every day when I got on the school bus.

In my early teens, I would read romance novels and lay in bed thinking about how I wanted to be seen deeply by someone. Whenever I was in airports, I would observe couples who were travelling together and wonder what it was like to take a vulnerable and exciting trip to a foreign world with someone you were so intimate with.

One of my favourite romantic fantasies was to imagine leaving my tiny town of 700 people for New York, where I would marry a Wall-Streeter and live in the countryside by the sea. He would travel to work, and I would stay home with our four kids and raise them until they found their own true love. We'd have the kind of Christmases you'd see in Hallmark romance movies: my now grown up kids would return with their spouses and children for a family reunion, and we'd all be merry and laugh together.

I'm such a romantic that my plantation style dreamhouse came right out of the movie, *The Notebook*. What a perfect backdrop for the perfect relationship with the perfect man I would one day meet and fall totally, perfectly in love with.

I spent years imagining every possible version of my fairytale future. I was only nineteen years old and hadn't had a lot of relationships except for my high school sweetheart; but I had a dream, a plan, and a million possible scenarios, which I was certain would now be fulfilled using the amazing tools of Access Consciousness.

I remember saying to Gary, "I want my prince to come and carry me off into the sunset on his white horse."

He looked straight at me and replied dryly:

"Julia, Prince Charming does not exist."

... Excuse me. What*?!*

I could almost hear the sound of my dreams shattering.

Convinced that Gary must be mistaken, I continued dating and searching for that prince. However, as I persisted, I couldn't help but notice that every single time, reality and fantasy never met.

So, I had to look a little (okay, a *lot*) closer at what Gary meant when he unceremoniously denounced my precious romantic visions.

I'd always sensed that having a relationship could be glorious, fun and expansive, but the choices I was making were not creating that. I realised that I'd made my ultimate happiness dependent on finding the perfect man and achieving the perfect relationship. Exhausting! And, as we've discussed before, any time you make *anyone* outside of you the source of your life, you are in trouble.

It became apparent to me that the degree of limitation I'd created by holding onto all the fairytales was quite astronomical. It forced me to question everything, and I wondered what I needed to choose that would give me what I actually desire?

Now, before you throw this book across the room and curse me for shattering your dreams as Gary once did to me, I am absolutely *not* telling you to give up the desire for a relationship or romance in your life. Romance is a fun, playful energy you can create and enjoy anytime and anywhere. You can live a fantastical and romantical life each day through your choice, regardless of your relationship status.

Creating your life includes creating *all kinds* of relationships that will contribute to you, especially to the relationship you have with you. Have you perhaps allowed your dreams and fantasies to limit your possibilities? What might be even greater than them?

I'd love to spend the rest of this chapter taking a look at what it might be like to create *everything* that would truly make you happy in the area of relationships, and see what magic shows up. Sound good?

RELATIONSHIP – THE BEST CHOICE. OR IS IT?

Relationship, and especially finding "The One" has been marketed as a superior position by just about everything and everyone. But after living in this world and meeting a lot of people, my impression is that many of us don't actually desire a relationship as commonly advertised. What if choosing to have a relationship isn't right and choosing not to have a relationship isn't wrong?

I believed a lot of things about relationships, until I actually had one and realised that I was going to have to "unlearn" everything I thought I knew if I wanted a chance of creating something great. In this chapter, I'm going to talk about both the energetic and pragmatic tools that have given me the ability to truly look at what I desired and what allowed it to show up. Let's get into it, because I'm kind of excited to see what can show up for you, too!

DO YOU TRULY DESIRE A RELATIONSHIP?

One of the coolest questions I never thought of asking myself before I heard it from Gary was:

Do I truly desire to have a relationship?

Relationship done by the rules of this world is usually full of a lot of crappiness instead of happiness. Growing up, I saw many relationships that were based on fulfilling expectations and judgements. In a fantasy fairytale, you get the perfect person that fulfills all your needs. In reality, when you do all those judgements and expectations, you end up creating separation and conflict rather than having the joy of exploring the contribution you can be to each other. My sense has always been that if I were going to have someone in my life, it should make my life and the other person's life greater. It should be expansive.

One way to know what choosing a relationship with someone would be like, is to ask a question. When I was considering marrying Anthony, I asked myself: "If I marry him, what will my life be like in 5, 10, 50, 100 years from now?" (Hint: asking for 5-100 years puts you in the energetic awareness of the choice, rather than letting you define it with your mind.) I perceived a powerful energy that matched the energy of the future I desire to have. I then asked, "If I don't marry him, what will my life be like?" The energy was dark, dim and not expansive. I trusted my knowing and chose to marry him. Does it mean life is "happily ever after" from that moment on? Nope. Does it mean we'll be married forever? Not necessarily. But in choosing to have Anthony and his kids in my life, I invited a universe of fun, contributive and creative energies that I get to be with each day, and that I am so grateful for.

I discovered something I hadn't anticipated really worked for me. For you, it could look very different, too. There is so much choice in this area and I'd like to give you some space to explore it more, so here is a fun little exercise to help you discover what you'd really enjoy.

EXERCISE: "WHAT WOULD WORK FOR ME?"

Here is a very pragmatic list of questions for discovering what would work for you in relationships:

- Do you like having sleepovers?
- Do you like people going through your fridge?

- Do you mind people rummaging through the stuff in your drawers?

If you like these things or they don't bother you, then a relationship can work for you. If you don't like sleepovers and dislike people going through your fridge or your things, then a relationship may not be your preference. Maybe having enjoyable part-time company or nice people to have sex with would be more fun? If you like people sleeping over sometimes, you could have a lover or lovers come and go! You could also have a relationship with someone and not live together. There are plenty of people who have very intimate relationships but live apart and visit each other's houses.

Another practical but important thing to consider is, if you are going to choose a relationship, and especially if you are going to live with that person, you have to be able to create a space you both enjoy. It should be easy and fun for you to live with this person!

One great tip I received from Gary about knowing if you could live with someone was this: *When you meet somebody and go into their house, how does it make you and your body feel? Does it feel warm and comfortable and energetically congruent? Do you share similar wavelengths of energy with them?*

The first time I went to visit Anthony's house it almost felt like going home. When his late wife passed away he redecorated everything himself, so that he and the kids could have a new energy for their future. It was a beautiful place and as soon as I walked in, I thought, "Oh, I could live with this person."

Having said that, when Anthony and I built our house and started creating our nest together, we didn't always agree on how we were going to decorate. Imagine two high-maintenance women arguing and fighting to get their own way! Luckily, with our similar taste and commitment to creating an elegant and cozy place to live, we eventually got there, and we continue to have fun creating our space.

A DIFFERENT RELATIONSHIP CHECKLIST

About a year before I met Anthony, my relationship question to the universe was:

What would it take to have some of the kindest, happiest, caring, most conscious beings in the universe in my everyday life?

When I started asking this, I had a kind of image show up in my mind of five people sitting around a table, but I couldn't really see who or what it was. I imagined it was perhaps a writer's group sharing creative thoughts or a theatre group writing a play together. I thought, "That would be cool!" but I didn't think much of it and kept going along my merry way.

Not long after Anthony and I started dating, I was having dinner with him and the kids. I suddenly realised, "Oh wait, this is the table! These are the five people!" Wow. That did not show up like I thought it would *at all.* I didn't even consider that the contributive beings could be kids.

This is what I love most about using energy to invite relationships: the surprising and greater-than-you-can-imagine magic that can show up. Most often, when asking for a relationship, people will list physical attributes they want and say things like, "He's got to be tall, handsome, with dark hair and eyes, have a good job, and go skiing with me in Colorado every winter." But these kinds of checklists really limit you because they are solely based on an image. They do not include the energetic attributes that would actually create a relationship that works for you. If I'd had a narrow checklist instead of my question, there would have been no space for Anthony and his kids to show up in my life.

Now, I'm not saying don't write a list! But if you do, base it on the energy. Write down the essential elements, which in my case were kind, happy, caring and conscious beings. And think about writing down your deal-breakers as well, for example, doing drugs would be a deal-breaker in a relationship for me, so I am aware of that when I am asking for what I desire.

And, there are a few energies in particular that I'd like to invite you to engage with so that they can contribute to you and your relationships in ways you might not have considered.

FIVE ENERGIES FOR ALL YOUR RELATIONSHIPS

The following energies are what I now consider "essential ingredients" to creating relationships. As you read this next part, please enjoy the gift of each of these energies, and really allow yourself to indulge in what prioritising them more will create for you.

The first energy I'd like to mention is *kindness.*

When someone has your back and treats you with kindness and respect, how do you handle that? If you look closely, you might not be as good at receiving kindness as you think.

If you are not in the habit of choosing kindness with yourself, not only will you fail to recognise when kindness comes to you, you'll refuse it dynamically, sending flaming arrows back to the person who was foolish enough to gift it to you. Sound crazy? Well, it is! And yet, that is how far we'll go to reject kindness.

I've done it often enough myself to know. In fact, I've lost count of the amount of times Gary had my back on a sticking point with Anthony, and rather than receive the kindness that Gary was being to both of us, I'd be dismissive of Gary, make Anthony the bad guy and me the perfect one, and basically go all out to burn their houses down.

I've also experienced being on the other side of that scenario – and it is likely you have, too! Have you ever been kind to someone who couldn't receive it and slammed it back in your face? It was not because you did something wrong, it is simply because you liked them more than they liked themselves, and they assumed you must be stupid, insane, or both, to treat them better than they treat themselves. And we do this without even realising we are doing it.

Rejecting kindness is a hardwired habit. To change it, you have to begin demanding that you be and have more kindness in your own world. And to keep choosing it, even when it's not easy!

When I'm uncomfortable about the amount of kindness being gifted to me, and I sense myself going into that pattern of grand rejection, I've learned to ask, "What kindness do I need to be with me, that would allow me to receive the kindness from others that I have decided I cannot have?"

Being and receiving kindness for you gets easier the more you choose it. And, if you are reading this right now thinking that you don't have a clue what true kindness is, ask the universe to show you – and do an energy pull! (Yes, it's that easy!) The hardest part of all of this is to commit to being kind to yourself, no matter what. Once you do, the universe will do everything it can to show you the kindness you can have.

The second energy is *nurturing*.

There is a beautiful simplicity to nurturing – it is a coziness that feeds your body and soul. If you were a plant, it would be the nourishment you receive from the rain and sun on your leaves, the soil around your roots, and the kind gardener who receives such delight and joy in tending to you. It is a beautiful energy that is available for anyone willing to receive it.

With Anthony, just nuzzling up together or doing daily activities while we joke and laugh, or watching him make up some hilarious skit about the amazing and unique way he sees the world, contributes so much lightness to my world. It really isn't more complicated than that.

Imagine what a relationship that would nurture your entire body and being would truly be like? In a relationship, what would it be like if just being yourselves with one another and simply enjoying each other nurtured and expanded your world?

The third energies are *humour and laughter*.

Have you noticed that if you lighten up and laugh, things that seemed so significant suddenly become irrelevant and melt away? Humour and laughter are amazing capacities that allow us to be more vulnerable. It relaxes our death-grip on rightness, which kills the joy in relationships faster than anything else.

When Anthony and I fight and both of us want to be right, it can be like a clash of the Titans, or maybe more of a melodrama. I'll admit that I actually *do* love a bit of drama in my life. Sometimes I just need my drama fix! And you know what? It's not wrong to realise you enjoy the rush you can get from it all. The key is, if you choose to create drama, at the very least, *enjoy* it. And if you desire a more peaceful co-existence, what if you could begin to infuse your drama with a sense of humour, so it becomes lighter and more playful, easier to change in the moment, and a lot less significant?

I recall one time in particular; I started to get really upset about something and was in a fit of hormonal crying, being super dramatic. Suddenly, I thought, "If I'm choosing this drama right now, I'm going to own it!" so I put on this retro-style wedding gown I had in my wardrobe, applied heavy mascara and ran all through the house, flailing around from mirror to mirror. I smeared the mascara down my face, mixing it with my tears until I looked like a full-on psycho-bride. It was fun and funny to watch myself do this, and turn my tears into laughter.

The fourth energy is *true caring*.

When Anthony and I first got together, one of the things I both loved, admired and, frankly, freaked out about was that he'd often "forget" to judge certain things. I kept thinking, "He should be more careful!" but what I really meant was, "He should judge more." Sometimes, I'd step in, attempt to do the judging for him and show him how and why he should judge something. Then I'd get annoyed with him for not getting it or for not choosing to change his perspective to match mine. After doing this continually and getting super exasperated, I had an epiphany: "Wait! I've been asking to have people in my life that create greater consciousness and kindness on the planet, yet when Anthony is being exactly that, I'm trying to stop it!" Anthony's unwillingness to judge was a true greatness, but I'd been treating it as a problem on the pretense that I was being protective and caring. I realised that true caring would be to have total gratitude for Anthony's difference in this area. I also noticed that by giving up my judgement of him, there was space for more relaxation and appreciation between us, as well as a greater peace in my own world.

The common practice of judging those we are most close to may feel like proof that we care about them, and they care about us. In practicality, it is a limiting perspective that hinders the true caring we can choose. When someone tries to control or change what you think or do, does it truly feel loving? When someone appreciates you exactly as you are, with no need for you to be any different, isn't that energy so attractive? What would it be like if you truly allowed yourself to be exactly who you are, and your loved ones to be exactly who they are, too? And… what if you asked for more people in your life who truly cared enough to never judge you and to be happy for you when you changed?

The fifth and last energy on this list is *curiosity*.

One time, Gary said to me, "You and Anthony should break up."

That man has a real knack for getting me to pay attention by saying all kinds of stuff most people would never say. And yet again, it worked. I was startled, "What do you mean by that?"

"What aren't you choosing for you because of your relationship?" was his next question.

I went through a quick mental list and realised there were quite a few things I had taken off the table for me since getting married. One of them was that I really wanted to travel and facilitate classes for weeks at a time, but my assumption was that I'd probably have to be single again to choose anything like that.

It was extra illuminating to have this awareness, because in truth I was already travelling and facilitating quite a lot, usually a week or two out of every month. But I'd put a limit on how much I could do so I could still take care of everything at home, and I'd been getting resentful of this role I'd taken while the same thing did not seem to apply to Anthony. Now that Gary had startled me into questioning my presumptions, I realised that nothing except my point of view was stopping me from doing it, especially not my marriage! Suddenly, my curiosity and enthusiasm for life began blossoming again, and I booked a phenomenal three-week trip to Europe, facilitating a bunch of classes and having way too much fun.

I recalled how much traveling contributes vitality and nourishment to my body and being, which in turn feeds all aspects of my life. I'd previously thought traveling more would be selfish and not honouring of my relationship, but it turns out the opposite was true.

Are there areas of life where you put yourself into "auto-pilot" or create roles and expectations of yourself that have nothing to do with what you'd really like to choose? Is it time to shake things up and re-engage yourself in a vibrant and continual adventure of actively living and choosing for you? Spend some time with yourself, asking yourself, *"If I could truly choose anything, what would I choose?"* Then, take action! Once you do, you might be surprised at how many people in your life will actively cheer you on and contribute to you along the way.

LEARNING TO RECEIVE IN WAYS YOU ARE NOT SUPPOSED TO RECEIVE

At the beginning of my relationship with Anthony, he was such a non-judgemental person who wanted to be madly in love with me. I, however, was not willing to let my guard down. I thought if I received all the adoration he had for me, it meant that I was weak. He had all this love to give, but I would set out to keep a distance and destroy it. I remember one time, we were walking to this amazing restaurant in Vancouver on a romantic date he'd planned, and I created a fight with him, saying, "You are just *so* into love. I think you need to find some hobbies other than love." You could almost hear his heart crushing. I mean, what a thing to say!

While doing insane things like this to diminish what Anthony was gifting me, I also recognised that he was different to anyone I'd had in my life – by a loooooong shot. He was present with me and seemed to have an unlimited resource of love to give, and I just did not know how to take it. I went through some major changes in order to receive it and him. At one point I looked back and realised there was almost no one I knew who was willing to have that detailed, intense level of intimacy. I had to increase my vulnerability dramatically to let this in.

It is totally, screamingly uncomfortable at times to receive a level of caring and nurturing from someone who doesn't judge you, even the parts of you that you try to hide because you think they are ugly. I've only ever been able to get past those moments and receive more from Anthony when I've allowed myself to be kinder to me.

One of the things I learned to do was allow Anthony to contribute to my life and to create our life together without giving myself up. At first, I thought being too "together" would make me lose myself totally. But as we continued our relationship, it became this dance of learning to receive more, to choose more, and to have each other's backs while being honest with ourselves about what we each need to choose to create lives that are joyful for us.

My relationship has also gifted my business, providing inspiration for my podcast and classes called, "As Trophy Wives, What is Required of Us?"

You might notice that Trophy Wife is a pretty judgement-loaded term. I remember watching a TV show as a kid, where a young blonde bimbo-acting character with big boobs was on screen, with this yucky but rich older husband, and the rest of the characters were secretly laughing at her and making jokes about her being a Trophy Wife. It looked like a very undesirable position to me, and I decided right then I would never become a Trophy Wife. Of course, I then became a woman in her early twenties who went from being totally independent to marrying a man twice her age and becoming a step-mom seemingly overnight. What do you think the judgement I received was?

Yep, Trophy Wife!

But instead of running away and hiding under a rock, I looked at it, and of course, asked Gary a question about it. He said, *"What if a trophy wife is just someone who is willing to be kind to her husband and not make him wrong, and won't make herself wrong either?"* This turned everything on its head and I started to excitedly create my podcast and classes, because I realised that underneath so many of these things that are judged as wrong, there is a treasure trove of possibility.

You don't have to be in a relationship to be a trophy wife. And it's not just wives. You can be a trophy daughter, a trophy sister, a trophy husband, a trophy father, brother, mother, friend, boss... you can be a trophy anything! Being a trophy-person is about honouring you, not lessening who you are and what you bring, and not making loved ones less either. It is a place of kindness and creation and learning to receive. That is a choice we all have, if we are willing to go beyond the judgements of what we've decided is acceptable, and to ask for more than we think is okay to receive.

ENERGY PULL #8: MORE MAGIC

What if you could receive far more than you are supposed to, including with your relationships? What if asking for more, receiving more, and enjoying more was the foundation of your life? Rembember in Chapter 9, we talked about hedonism – the willingness to have the pleasure, joy and sweetness of life and living? A huge part of that is being willing to keep asking for more and greater, and then welcoming it with open arms as it shows up.

The times I have allowed myself to ask for and have more than I was ever supposed to have, have sometimes felt akin to walking naked and totally exposed in the world. But every time I have been willing to be kinder to myself, to pursue my life as the hedonist I truly am, with my exuberance and curiosity for greater, I will pull rivers, waterfalls and oceans of contribution into my life. And it is so fun!

I've seen time and time again how changing my energy truly changes everything. Using the energy pulls is one of my favourite ways to tell the universe, "Hey, I'm changing this, I'm choosing this, who and what will join the party with me and make it even greater?"

Now it's time for the last energy pull in the book, which is really just the beginning of being more of the magic you truly are:

1. Relax and expand your energy beyond your body into the playful, sparkling expanses of the universe.

2. Indulge in the energies of:

    - *Waking up every day, with no thoughts in your head, holding onto nothing from yesterday, just a pervasive sense of curiosity and excitement for what is possible, knowing that to have what you desire, all you need to do is to choose it.*

    - *Being so happy to be yourself in every moment that you never again muster up a single judgement of you.*

    - *Asking for – and receiving – everything you desire as you go throughout your day, with total ease.*

    - *Being nurtured and cared for by everything and everyone you encounter.*

- *What would it be like to receive that much contribution in a day? What if, no matter the amount of magic that shows up today, tomorrow, you will ask and receive even more?*

3. Put all those energies into an energy bubble in front of you. Pull from all over the universe, from every direction, through you and through the energy bubble.

4. When your heart area warms up or expands a little, slightly reverse the flow and let trickles go back to everything that matches that energy, so it can find you and show up for you in all kinds of amazing and surprising ways.

5. Then reverse the flow, and pull energy once again, through the universe, through the bubble, through your body, and out into the universe.

Take a moment to be grateful and in wonderment of you. What magic can and will you create? How much fun, question and change have you already created while playing with this book, and how much more of everything that you desire can you now invite into your world?

(THIS IS MORE OF A POSTSCRIPT THAN A RECAP)

I hope this chapter has given you an avenue to truly explore and become more willing than ever to ask for (and receive) whatever it is that you'd like.

What would it be like to have a phenomenal relationship with yourself, where you continually create greater, no matter what?

What if you could have more kindness, nurturing, caring, humour, fun and ease in your life? The universe truly desires for you to have it all. And the world certainly needs you to be these energies more than ever.

THIS IS THE LAST PAGE (BUT NOT THE END!)

Woohoo! You made it to the last page (or maybe you flipped here first, looking for spoilers before deciding if you'll go back and read the rest of the book. A perfectly respectable strategy!)

If you've read through this book already, or parts of it, do you feel a little different from when you started? Do you have a sense of new possibilities about what you are capable of, what you truly desire, and how much more fun and magic you can have as you live and create?

And truly, this is just the beginning. The first energy pull I ever did, I did it for 90 days. If you play with all the tools in this book over and over, how much can change and how much expansion of your life could you invite?

As far as I'm aware, life truly is meant to be a glorious adventure. And of course things aren't always easy, or comfortable, but there is a space of play and creation that we can come to any time, over and over again, where nothing has to be limited, nothing is impossible, and there is always, *always,* more.

If you'd like to continue using these tools, come find me here: juliasotas.com/arecipeformagic

For now, this is me, Julia, that really fucking weird person you've been hanging out with for a little while, saying thank you for joining me on this adventure, and I hope to meet you in person one day!

What can you do today that would make you happy right away?

RESOURCES FOR FUTURE MAGIC

Being You Changing the World, by Dr. Dain Heer
beingyouchangingtheworld.com

Body Whispering by Dr. Dain Heer
bodywhispererbook.com

Julia's website with all classes & events
juliasotas.com

Julia's Youtube Channel
YouTube.com/juliasotas

Julia's Instagram Page
instagram.com/juliasotas

If you would like to host Julia around the world for a class you can visit: juliasotas.com/contact

Access Consciousness Website
accessconsciousness.com

www.ingramcontent.com/pod-product-compliance
Lightning Source LLC
LaVergne TN
LVHW030912080826
845145LV00010B/2871
9781634937566